ALSO BY EVE ENSLER

Necessary Targets

The Good Body

Insecure at Last

I Am an Emotional Creature

In the Body of the World

EDITED BY EVE ENSLER
AND MOLLIE DOYLE

A Memory, a Monologue,
a Rant, and a Prayer

THE VAGINA MONOLOGUES

THE VAGINA MONOLOGUES

Eve Ensler

Foreword by Jacqueline Woodson
Afterword by Monique Wilson

BALLANTINE BOOKS

NEW YORK

2018 Ballantine Books Trade Paperback Edition

Published in the United States by Ballantine Books, an imprint of Random House, a division of Penguin Random House LLC, New York.

BALLANTINE and the HOUSE colophon are registered trademarks of Penguin Random House LLC.

Earlier editions of this book were originally published in hardcover in 1998 and 2008 and in trade paperback in 2001 and 2008 in the United States by Villard Books, an imprint of Random House, a division of Penguin Random House LLC.

Originally produced by HOME for Contemporary Theatre and Art at HERE, Randy Rollison, artistic director, and Barbara Busackino, producing director, in association with Wendy Evans Joseph. Produced Off-Broadway by David Stone, Willa Shalit, Nina Essman, Dan Markley/Mike Skipper, and the Araca Group.

The introduction by Eve Ensler was originally published as "Even with a Misogynist Predator-in-Chief, We Will Not be Silenced" in *The Guardian*, August 23, 2017.

LIBRARY OF CONGRESS CATALOGING-IN-PUBLICATION DATA
Ensler, Eve.
The vagina monologues / Eve Ensler
p. cm.
ISBN 978-0-399-18009-5
Ebook ISBN 978-0-375-50658-1
1. Monologues. 2. Vagina. 3. Women.
PS3555.N75V3 2001
812.54—dc21 00-043844

Printed in the United States of America on acid-free paper

randomhousebooks.com

6 8 9 7 5

Book design by Caroline Cunningham

For all the women who moan and matter

FOREWORD

Jacqueline Woodson

So needed back then—this book.

So needed. Right now—this book.

There is a spiritual that begins *There is a balm in Gilead to make the wounded whole. There is a balm in Gilead to heal the sin-sick soul.* For so many of us, coming of age in the fifties, sixties, seventies, and eighties, there were no balms. We moved through the world in our bodies filled with a sense of shame simply by virtue of being born with vaginas and breasts, hips and thighs. We didn't know the extent of the shame—where it had begun, by what grace we had come to know it. After all, hadn't the feminist movement changed the world for women? Hadn't we reclaimed our bodies, ourselves, and moved on?

Maybe. But . . .

The first time I read *The Vagina Monologues,* I was in my thirties, new to motherhood, with an infant daughter. The monologues on paper, as they had years before onstage, made me laugh, cry, happy-dance. But this time, there was something more—they made me think of my own past and my daughter's future. In reading the monologues, I realized that what had been missing from so many of our lives was the conversation and the celebration—the shameless celebration of vaginas and periods, breasts and butts and thighs. I knew that this conversation and celebration were going to be a part of my own daughter's life—and the lives of the many young people I would be a part of helping to raise.

There is a balm in Gilead to make the wounded whole.

The first time I got my period, I wished it away—successfully for another year. As a child I knew it only as "the curse" and truly felt cursed to suddenly have to deal with my bleeding, my body, the changes to it that were so visible to the world. A generation later, the first time my daughter got her period, she shouted, "Call the aunties! It's time for a celebration!"

Let's keep this conversation and this celebration going on!

INTRODUCTION TO THE 20TH ANNIVERSARY EDITION

Eve Ensler

The first time I ever performed *The Vagina Monologues,* I was sure somebody would shoot me. It might be hard to believe, but at that time, twenty years ago, no one said the word "vagina." Not in schools. Not on TV. Not even at the gynecologist. When mothers bathed their daughters, they referred to their vaginas as "pookis" or "poochis" or "down there." So when I stood onstage in a tiny theater in downtown Manhattan to deliver the monologues I had written about vaginas—after interviewing more than two hundred women—it felt as if I were pushing through an invisible barrier and breaching a very deep taboo.

But I did not get shot. At the end of each show of *The Vagina Monologues* there would be long lines of women who wanted to talk to me. At first, I thought they would want to share stories of desire and sexual satisfaction—the focus of a big part of the show. But they were lining up to anxiously tell me how and when they had been raped, or assaulted, or beaten, or molested. I was shocked to see that once the taboo was breached, it released a torrent of memories, anger, and sorrow.

And then something I could never have expected took place. The show was picked up by women all over the world who wanted to break the silence in their own communities about their bodies and their lives.

Memory one. Oklahoma City, the very heart

of the Republican heartland. A tiny warehouse. The second night, word has gotten out about the play and there are too many people and not enough seats, so people arrive with their own lawn chairs. I am performing under what is essentially a lightbulb. In the middle of a monologue, there is a great scuttling in the crowd. A young woman has fainted. I stop the play. The audience takes care of the woman, fanning her and getting her water. She stands up and declares what the play has emboldened her to say, for the first time: "I was raped by my stepfather." The audience hugs her and holds her as she weeps. Then, at her request, I continue with the show.

Memory two. Islamabad, Pakistan. The show is banned. So I attend an underground production of *The Vagina Monologues* where brave Pakistani actors are performing the play in secret. There are women who have come all the way from Taliban Afghanistan in the audience. Men are not allowed to sit in the audience, but instead sit in the back, behind a white curtain. During the performance, women cry and laugh so hard their chadors fall off.

Memory three. Mostar, Bosnia. The performance is to commemorate the restoration of the Mostar bridge, which was destroyed in the war. The crowd is composed of both Croats and Bosnians, who have been slaughtering one another so recently, and there is tension and uncertainty. Women read a monologue about the rape of women in Bosnia. The audience weeps, wails, screams out. The actors stop. Audience members console one another, hold one another and weep together—Croats holding Bosnians, and vice versa. The play resumes.

Memory four. Lansing, Michigan. Lisa Brown, a state representative, is reproached and silenced by the state legislature for using the word "vagina" in protesting a proposed bill restricting abortion. You are not allowed, she is told, to say that word. Two days later I fly out to Lansing and join Lisa and ten female house members on the steps of the statehouse for an emergency performance of *The Vagina Monologues*. Close to five thousand women attend, demanding that our body parts be named and recognized in our own democratic institutions. The taboo is broken. We can speak and be seen.

Shortly after the play was launched, with a group of other feminists, I helped form a movement called V-Day, to stand with all the women (cisgender, transgender, and gender-nonconforming, in all our colors) who were carrying out these fights across the world. Since then V-Day activists, through their productions of the monologues, have raised more than $100 million to support centers and shelters for rape and violence survivors, to fund hotlines, to confront rape culture.

And now, twenty years later, I wish for nothing more than to be able to say that radical antiracist feminists have won. But patriarchy, alongside white supremacy, is a recurrent virus. It lives dormant in the body politic and is activated by toxic predatory conditions. Certainly in the United States, with an openly racist and misogynist predator in chief, we are in the midst of a massive outbreak. Our job, until a cure is found, is to create hyperresistant conditions that build our immunity and our courage, making more outbreaks impossible. It starts where *The Vagina Monologues,* and so many other acts of radical feminist resistance, begin—by speaking out. By saying what we see. By refusing to be silenced.

They tried to stop us even saying the names of some of the most precious parts of our bodies. But here's what I learned. If something isn't named, it is not seen, it doesn't exist. Now more than ever, it's time to tell the crucial stories and say the words, whether they're "vagina," "My stepfather raped me," or "The president is a predator and a racist."

When you break the silence you realize how many other people were waiting for permission to do the same thing. We—every sort and type of woman, every single one of us, and our vaginas—will never be silenced again.

CONTENTS

Foreword by Jacqueline Woodson ix

Introduction to the 20th Anniversary Edition by Eve Ensler xiii

Preface xxi

The Vagina Monologues 1

Spotlight Monologues 91

V-Day 167

Say It, Stage It: V-Day at Twenty 169

V-Day Mission Statement 209

The 10 Guiding Principles of City of Joy 211

Afterword by Monique Wilson 213

Acknowledgments 229

PREFACE

"Vagina." There, I've said it. "Vagina"—said it again. I've been saying that word over and over for the last three years. I've been saying it in theaters, at colleges, in living rooms, in cafés, at dinner parties, on radio programs all over the country. I would be saying it on TV if someone would let me. I say it one hundred and twenty-eight times every evening I perform my show, *The Vagina Monologues,* which is based on interviews with a diverse group of more than two hundred women about their vaginas. I say it in my sleep. I say it because I'm not supposed to say it. I say it because it's an invisible word—a word that stirs up anxiety, awkwardness, contempt, and disgust.

I say it because I believe that what we don't say we don't see, acknowledge, or remember. What we don't say becomes a secret, and secrets often create shame and fear and myths. I say it because I want to someday feel comfortable saying it, and not ashamed and guilty.

I say it because we haven't come up with a word that's more inclusive, that really describes the entire area and all its parts. "Pussy" is probably a better word, but it has so much baggage connected with it. And besides, I don't think most of us have a clear idea of what we're talking about when we say "pussy." "Vulva" is a good word; it speaks more specifically, but I don't think most of us are clear what the vulva includes.

I say "vagina" because when I started saying it I discovered how fragmented I was, how disconnected my body was from my mind. My vagina was something over there, away in the distance. I rarely lived inside it, or even visited. I was busy working, writing; being a mother, a friend. I did not see my vagina as my primary resource, a place of sustenance, humor, and creativity. It was fraught there, full of fear. I'd been raped as a little girl, and although I'd grown up, and done all the adult things one does with one's vagina, I had never really reentered that part of my body after I'd been violated. I had essentially lived most of my life without my motor, my center, my second heart.

I say "vagina" because I want people to respond, and they have. They have tried to censor the word wherever *The Vagina Monologues* has traveled and in every form of communication: in ads in major newspapers, on tickets sold in department stores, on banners that hang in front of theaters, on box-office phone machines where the voice says only "Monologues" or "V. Monologues."

"Why is this?" I ask. " 'Vagina' is not a pornographic word; it's actually a medical word, a term for a body part, like 'elbow,' 'hand,' or 'rib.' "

"It may not be pornographic," people say, "but it's dirty. What if our little daughters were to hear it, what would we tell them?"

"Maybe you could tell them that they have a vagina," I say. "If they don't already know it. Maybe you could celebrate that."

"But we don't call their vaginas 'vagina,' " they say.

"What do you call them?" I ask.

And they tell me: "pooki," "poochie," "poope," "peepe poopelu" . . . and the list goes on and on.

I say "vagina" because I have read the statistics, and bad things are happening to women's vaginas everywhere: 500,000 women are raped every year in the United States; 100 million women have been genitally mutilated worldwide; and the list goes on and on. I say "vagina" because I want these bad things to stop. I know they will not stop until we acknowledge that they're going on, and the only way to make that possible is to enable women to talk without fear of punishment or retribution.

It's scary saying the word. "Vagina." At first it feels like you're crashing through an invisible wall. "Vagina." You feel guilty and wrong, as if someone's going to strike you down. Then, after you say the word the hundredth time or the thousandth time, it occurs to you that it's *your* word, *your* body, *your* most essential place. You suddenly realize that all the shame and embarrassment you've previously felt saying the word has been a form of silencing your desire, eroding your ambition.

Then you begin to say the word more and more. You say it with a kind of passion, a kind of urgency, because you sense that if you stop saying it, the fear will overcome you again and you will fall back into an embarrassed whisper. So you say it everywhere you can, bring it up in every conversation.

You're excited about your vagina; you want to study it and explore it and introduce yourself to it, and find out how to listen to it, and give it pleasure, and keep it healthy and wise and strong. You learn how to satisfy yourself and teach your lover how to satisfy you.

You're aware of your vagina all day, wherever you are—in your car, at the supermarket, at the gym, in the office. You're aware of this precious, gorgeous, life-bearing part of you between your legs, and it makes you smile; it makes you proud.

And as more women say the word, saying it becomes less of a big deal; it becomes part of our language, part of our lives. Our vaginas become integrated and respected and sacred. They become part of our bodies, connected to our minds, fueling our spirits. And the shame leaves and the violation stops, because vaginas are visible and real, and they are connected to powerful, wise, vagina-talking women.

We have a huge journey in front of us.

This is the beginning. Here's the place to think about our vaginas, to learn about other women's vaginas, to hear stories and interviews, to answer questions and to ask them. Here's the place to release the myths, shame, and fear. Here's the place to practice saying the word, because, as we know, the word is what propels us and sets us free. "VAGINA."

THE VAGINA MONOLOGUES

I bet you're worried. *I* was worried. That's why I began this piece. I was worried about vaginas. I was worried about what we think about vaginas, and even more worried that we don't think about them. I was worried about my own vagina. It needed a context of other vaginas—a community, a culture of vaginas. There's so much darkness and secrecy surrounding them—like the Bermuda Triangle. Nobody ever reports back from there.

In the first place, it's not so easy even to find your vagina. Women go weeks, months, sometimes years without looking at it. I interviewed a high-powered businesswoman who told me she was too busy; she didn't have the time. Looking at your vagina, she said, is a full day's work. You have to get down there on your back in front of a mirror that's standing on its own, full-length preferred. You've got to get in the perfect position, with the perfect light, which then is shadowed somehow by the mirror and the angle you're at. You get all twisted up. You're arching your head up, killing your back. You're exhausted by then. She said she didn't have the time for that. She was busy.

So I decided to talk to women about their vaginas, to do vagina interviews, which became vagina monologues. I talked with over two hundred women. I talked to older women, young women, married women, single women, lesbians, college professors, actors, corporate professionals, sex workers, African American women, Hispanic women, Asian American women, Native American women, Caucasian women, Jewish women. At first women were reluctant to talk. They were a little shy. But once they got going, you couldn't stop them. Women secretly love to talk about their vaginas. They get very excited, mainly because no one's ever asked them before.

Let's just start with the word "vagina." It sounds like an infection at best, maybe a medical instrument: "Hurry, Nurse, bring me the vagina." "Vagina." "Vagina." Doesn't matter how many times you say it, it never sounds like a word you want to say. It's a totally ridiculous, completely unsexy word. If you use it during sex, trying to be politically correct—"Darling, could you stroke my vagina?"—you kill the act right there.

I'm worried about vaginas, what we call them and don't call them.

In Great Neck, they call it a pussycat. A woman there told me that her mother used to tell her, "Don't wear panties underneath your pajamas, dear; you need to air out your pussycat." In

Westchester they called it a pooki, in New Jersey a twat. There's "powderbox," "derrière," a "poochi," a "poopi," a "peepe," a "poopelu," a "poonani," a "pal" and a "piche," "toadie," "dee dee," "nishi," "dignity," "monkey box," "coochi snorcher," "cooter," "labbe," "Gladys Siegelman," "VA," "wee wee," "horsespot," "nappy dugout," "mongo," a "pajama," "fannyboo," "mushmellow," a "ghoulie," "possible," "tamale," "tottita," "Connie," a "Mimi" in Miami, "split knish" in Philadelphia, and "schmende" in the Bronx. I am worried about vaginas.

HAIR

You cannot love a vagina unless you love hair. Many people do not love hair. My first and only husband hated hair. He said it was cluttered and dirty. He made me shave my vagina. It looked puffy and exposed and like a little girl. This excited him. When he made love to me, my vagina felt the way a beard must feel. It felt good to rub it, and painful. Like scratching a mosquito bite. It felt like it was on fire. There were screaming red bumps. I refused to shave it again. Then my husband had an affair. When we went to marital therapy, he said he screwed around because I wouldn't please him sexually. I wouldn't shave my vagina. The therapist had a thick German accent and gasped between sentences to show her empathy. She asked me why I didn't want to please my husband. I told her I thought it was weird. I felt little when my hair was gone down there, and I couldn't help talking in a baby voice, and the skin got irritated and even calamine lotion wouldn't help it. She told me marriage was a compromise. I asked her if shaving my vagina would stop him from screwing around. I asked her if she'd had many cases like this before. She said that questions diluted the process. I needed to jump in. She was sure it was a good beginning.

This time, when we got home, he got to shave my vagina. It was like a therapy bonus prize. He clipped it a few times, and there was a little blood in the bathtub. He didn't even notice it, 'cause he was so happy shaving me. Then, later, when my husband was pressing against me, I could feel his spiky sharpness sticking into me, my naked puffy vagina. There was no protection. There was no fluff.

I realized then that hair is there for a reason—it's the leaf around the flower, the lawn around the house. You have to love hair in order to love the vagina. You can't pick the parts you want. And besides, my husband never stopped screwing around.

"If your vagina got dressed, what would it wear?"

A beret.

A leather jacket.

Silk stockings.

Mink.

A pink boa.

A male tuxedo.

Jeans.

Something formfitting.
Emeralds.
An evening gown.
Sequins.
Armani only.
A tutu.
See-through black underwear.
A taffeta ball gown.
Something machine washable.
Costume eye mask.
Purple velvet pajamas.
Angora.
A red bow.
Ermine and pearls.
A large hat full of flowers.
A leopard hat.
A silk kimono.
Glasses.
Sweatpants.
A tattoo.
An electrical shock device to keep unwanted
strangers away.

High heels.

Lace *and* combat boots.

Purple feathers and twigs and shells.

Cotton.

A pinafore.

A bikini.

A slicker.

"If your vagina could talk, what would it say, in two words?"

Slow down.
Is that you?
Feed me.
I want.
Yum, yum.
Oh, yeah.

Start again.
No, over there.
Lick me.
Stay home.
Brave choice.
Think again.
More, please.
Embrace me.
Let's play.
Don't stop.
More, more.
Remember me?
Come inside.
Not yet.
Whoah, Mama.
Yes yes.
Rock me.
Enter at your own risk.
Oh, God.
Thank God.
I'm here.
Let's go.

Let's go.

Find me.

Thank you.

Bonjour.

Too hard.

Don't give up.

Where's Brian?

That's better.

Yes, there. There.

THE FLOOD

[Jewish, Queens accent]

Down there? I haven't been down there since 1953. No, it had nothing to do with Eisenhower. No, no, it's a cellar down there. It's very damp, clammy. You don't want to go down there. Trust me. You'd get sick. Suffocating. Very nauseating. The smell of the clamminess and the mildew and everything. Whew! Smells unbearable. Gets in your clothes.

No, there was no accident down there. It

didn't blow up or catch on fire or anything. It wasn't so dramatic. I mean . . . well, never mind. No. Never mind. I can't talk to you about this. What's a smart girl like you going around talking to old ladies about their down-theres for? We didn't do this kind of a thing when I was a girl. What? Jesus, okay.

There was this boy, Andy Leftkov. He was cute—well, I thought so. And tall, like me, and I really liked him. He asked me out for a date in his car. . . .

I can't tell you this. I can't do this, talk about down there. You just know it's there. Like the cellar. There's rumbles down there sometimes. You can hear the pipes, and things get caught there, little animals and things, and it gets wet, and sometimes people have to come and plug up the leaks. Otherwise, the door stays closed. You forget about it. I mean, it's part of the house, but you don't see it or think about it. It has to be there, though, 'cause every house needs a cellar. Otherwise the bedroom would be in the basement.

Oh, Andy, Andy Leftkov. Right. Andy was very good-looking. He was a catch. That's what we called it in my day. We were in his car, a new white Chevy BelAir. I remember thinking that my legs were too long for the seat. I have long legs. They were bumping up against the dashboard. I was looking at my big kneecaps when he just kissed me in this surprisingly "Take me by control like they do in the movies" kind of way. And I got excited, so excited, and, well, there was a flood down there. I couldn't control it. It was like this force of passion, this river of life just flooded out of me, right through my panties, right onto the car seat of his new white Chevy BelAir. It wasn't pee and it was smelly—well, frankly, I didn't really smell anything at all, but he said, Andy said, that it smelled like sour milk and it was staining his car seat. I was "a stinky weird girl," he said. I wanted to explain that his kiss had caught me off guard, that I wasn't normally like this. I tried to wipe the flood up with my dress. It was a new yellow primrose dress and it looked so ugly with the flood on it. Andy drove me home and he never, never said another word and when I got out and closed his car door, I closed the whole store. Locked it. Never opened for business again. I dated some after that, but the idea of flooding made me too nervous. I never even got close again.

I used to have dreams, crazy dreams. Oh, they're dopey. Why? Burt Reynolds. I don't know why. He never did much for me in life, but in my dreams . . . it was always Burt and I. Burt and I. Burt and I. We'd be out. Burt and I. It was some restaurant like the kind you see in Atlantic City, all big with chandeliers and stuff and thousands of waiters with vests on. Burt would give me this orchid corsage. I'd pin it on my blazer. We'd laugh. We were always laughing, Burt and I. Eat shrimp cocktail. Huge shrimp, fabulous shrimp. We'd laugh more. We were very happy together. Then he'd look into my eyes and pull me to him in the middle of the restaurant—and, just as he was about to kiss me, the room would start to shake, pigeons would fly out from under the table—I don't know what those pigeons were doing there—and the flood would come straight from down there. It would pour out of me. It would pour and pour. There would be fish inside it, and little boats, and the whole restaurant would fill with water, and Burt would be standing knee-deep in my flood, looking horribly disappointed in me that I'd done it again, horrified as he watched his friends, Dean Martin and the like, swim past us in their tuxedos and evening gowns.

I don't have those dreams anymore. Not since they took away just about everything connected with down there. Moved out the uterus, the tubes, the whole works. The doctor thought he was being funny. He told me if you don't use it, you lose it. But really I found out it was cancer. Everything around it had to go. Who needs it, anyway? Right? Highly overrated. I've done other things. I love the dog shows. I sell antiques.

What would it wear? What kind of question

is that? What would it wear? It would wear a big sign:

"Closed Due to Flooding."

What would it say? I told you. It's not like that. It's not like a person who speaks. It stopped being a thing that talked a long time ago. It's a place. A place you don't go. It's closed up, under the house. It's down there. You happy? You made me talk—you got it out of me. You got an old lady to talk about her down-there. You feel better now? [Turns away; turns back.]

You know, actually, you're the first person I ever talked to about this, and I feel a little better.

VAGINA FACT

"At a witch trial in 1593, the investigating lawyer (a married man) apparently discovered a clitoris for the first time; [he] identified it as a devil's teat, sure proof of the witch's guilt. It was 'a little lump of flesh, in manner sticking out as if it had been a teat, to the length of half an inch,' which the gaoler, 'perceiving at the first sight thereof, meant not to disclose, because it was adjoining to so secret a place which was not decent to be seen. Yet in the end, not willing to conceal so strange a matter,' he showed it to various bystanders. The bystanders had never seen anything like it. The witch was convicted."

—*The Woman's Encyclopedia of Myths and Secrets*

I WAS TWELVE. MY MOTHER SLAPPED ME.

Second grade, seven years old, my brother was talking about periods. I didn't like the way he was laughing.

I went to my mother. "What's a period?" I said. "It's punctuation," she said. "You put it at the end of a sentence."

My father brought me a card: "To my little girl who isn't so little anymore."

I was terrified. My mother showed me the

thick sanitary napkins. I was to bring the used ones to the can under the kitchen sink.

I remember being one of the last. I was thirteen.

We all wanted it to come.

I was so afraid. I started putting the used pads in brown paper bags in the dark storage places under the roof.

Eighth grade. My mother said, "Oh, that's nice."

In junior high—brown drips before it came. Coincided with a little hair under my arms, which grew unevenly: one armpit had hair, the other didn't.

I was sixteen, sort of scared.

My mother gave me codeine. We had bunk beds. I went down and lay there. My mother was so uncomfortable.

One night, I came home late and snuck into bed without turning on any lights. My mother had found the used pads and put them between the sheets of my bed.

I was twelve years old, still in my underpants. Hadn't gotten dressed. Looked down on the staircase. There it was.

Looked down and I saw blood.

Seventh grade; my mother sort of noticed my underwear. Then she gave me plastic diapers.

My mom was very warm—"Let's get you a pad."

My friend Marcia, they celebrated when she got hers. They had dinner for her.

We all wanted our period.

We all wanted it *now*.

Thirteen years old. It was before Kotex. Had to watch your dress. I was black and poor. Blood on the back of my dress in church. Didn't show, but I was guilty.

I was ten and a half. No preparation. Brown gunk on my underpants.

She showed me how to put in a tampon. Only got in halfway.

I associated my period with inexplicable phenomena.

My mother told me I had to use a rag. My mother said no to tampons. You couldn't put anything in your sugar dish.

Wore wads of cotton. Told my mother. She gave me Elizabeth Taylor paper dolls.

Fifteen years old. My mother said, "Mazel tov." She slapped me in the face. Didn't know if it was a good thing or a bad thing.

My period, like cake mix before it's baked. Indians sat on moss for five days. Wish I were Native American.

I was fifteen and I'd been hoping to get it. I was tall and I kept growing.

When I saw white girls in the gym with tampons, I thought they were bad girls.

Saw little red drops on the pink tiles. I said, "Yeah."

My mom was glad for me.

Used OB and liked putting my fingers up there.

Eleven years old, wearing white pants. Blood started to come out.

Thought it was dreadful.

I'm not ready.

I got back pains.

I got horny.

Twelve years old. I was happy. My friend had a Ouija board, asked when we were going to get our periods, looked down, and I saw blood.

Looked down and there it was.

I'm a woman.

Terrified.

Never thought it would come.

Changed my whole feeling about myself. I became very silent and mature. A good Vietnamese woman—quiet worker, virtuous, never speaks.

Nine and a half. I was sure I was bleeding to death, rolled up my underwear and threw them in a corner. Didn't want to worry my parents.

My mother made me hot water and wine, and I fell asleep.

I was in my bedroom in my mother's apartment. I had a comic book collection. My mother said, "You mustn't lift your box of comic books."

My girlfriends told me you hemorrhage every month.

My mother was in and out of mental hospitals. She couldn't take me coming of age.

"Dear Miss Carling, Please excuse my daughter from basketball. She has just matured."

At camp they told me not to take a bath with my period. They wiped me down with antiseptic.

Scared people would smell it. Scared they'd say I smelled like fish.

Throwing up, couldn't eat.

I got hungry.

Sometimes it's very red.

I like the drops that drop into the toilet. Like paint.

Sometimes it's brown and it disturbs me.

I was twelve. My mother slapped me and brought me a red cotton shirt. My father went out for a bottle of sangria.

THE VAGINA WORKSHOP

[A slight English accent]

My vagina is a shell, a round pink tender shell, opening and closing, closing and opening. My vagina is a flower, an eccentric tulip, the center acute and deep, the scent delicate, the petals gentle but sturdy.

I did not always know this. I learned this in the vagina workshop. I learned this from a woman who runs the vagina workshop, a woman who believes in vaginas, who really sees vaginas, who helps women see their own vaginas by seeing other women's vaginas.

In the first session the woman who runs the vagina workshop asked us to draw a picture of our own "unique, beautiful, fabulous vagina." That's what she called it. She wanted to know what our own unique, beautiful, fabulous vagina looked like to us. One woman who was pregnant drew a big red mouth screaming with coins spilling out. Another very skinny woman drew a big serving plate with a kind of Devonshire pattern on it. I drew a huge black dot with little squiggly lines around it. The black dot was equal to a black hole in space, and the squiggly lines were meant to be people or things or just your basic atoms that got lost there. I had always thought of my vagina as an anatomical vacuum randomly sucking up particles and objects from the surrounding environment.

I had always perceived my vagina as an independent entity, spinning like a star in its own galaxy, eventually burning up on its own gaseous energy or exploding and splitting into thousands of other smaller vaginas, all of them then spinning in their own galaxies.

I did not think of my vagina in practical or biological terms. I did not, for example, see it as a part of my body, something between my legs, attached to me.

In the workshop we were asked to look at our vaginas with hand mirrors. Then, after careful examination, we were to verbally report to the group what we saw. I must tell you that up until this point everything I knew about my vagina was based on hearsay or invention. I had never really seen the thing. It had never occurred to me to look at it. My vagina existed for me on some abstract plane. It seemed so reductive and awkward to look at it, getting down there the way we did in the workshop, on our shiny blue mats, with our hand mirrors. It reminded me of how the early astronomers must have felt with their primitive telescopes.

I found it quite unsettling at first, my vagina.

Like the first time you see a fish cut open and you discover this other bloody complex world inside, right under the skin. It was so raw, so red, so fresh. And the thing that surprised me most was all the layers. Layers inside layers, opening into more layers.

My vagina amazed me. I couldn't speak when it came my turn in the workshop. I was speechless. I had awakened to what the woman who ran the workshop called "vaginal wonder." I just wanted to lie there on my mat, my legs spread, examining my vagina forever.

It was better than the Grand Canyon, ancient and full of grace. It had the innocence and freshness of a proper English garden. It was funny, very funny. It made me laugh. It could hide and seek, open and close. It was a mouth. It was the morning.

Then, the woman who ran the workshop asked how many women in the workshop had had orgasms. Two women tentatively raised their hands. I didn't raise my hand, but I had had orgasms. I didn't raise my hand because they were accidental orgasms. They happened *to* me. They happened in my dreams, and I would wake in splendor. They happened a lot in water, mostly in the bath. Once in Cape Cod. They happened on horses, on bicycles, on the treadmill at the gym. I did not raise my hand because although I had had orgasms, I did not know how to make one happen. I had never tried to make one happen. I thought it was a mystical, magical thing. I didn't want to interfere. It felt wrong, getting involved—contrived, manipulative. It felt Hollywood. Orgasms by formula. The surprise would be gone, and the mystery. The problem, of course, was that the surprise had been gone for two years. I hadn't had a magical accidental orgasm in a long time, and I was frantic. That's why I was in the workshop.

And then the moment had arrived that I both dreaded and secretly longed for. The woman who ran the workshop asked us to take out our hand mirrors again and to see if we could locate our clitoris. We were there, the group of us women, on our backs, on our mats, finding our spots, our locus, our reason, and I don't know why, but I started crying. Maybe it was sheer embarrassment. Maybe it was knowing that I had to give up the fantasy, the enormous life-consuming fantasy, that someone or something was going to do this for me—the fantasy that someone was coming to lead my life, to choose direction, to give me orgasms. I was used to living off the record, in a magical, superstitious way. This clitoris finding, this wild workshop on shiny blue mats, was making the whole thing real, too real. I could feel the panic coming. The simultaneous terror and realization that I had avoided finding my clitoris, had rationalized it as mainstream and consumerist because I was, in fact, terrified that I did not *have* a clitoris, terrified that I was one of those constitutionally incapables, one of those frigid, dead, shut-down, dry, apricot-tasting, bitter—oh, my God. I lay there with my mirror looking for my spot, reaching with my fingers, and all I could think about was the time when I was ten and lost my gold ring with the emeralds in a lake. How I kept diving over and over to the bottom of the lake, running my hands over stones and fish and bottle caps and slimy stuff, but never my ring. The panic I felt. I knew I'd be punished. I shouldn't have worn it swimming.

The woman who ran the workshop saw my insane scrambling, sweating, and heavy breathing. She came over. I told her, "I've lost my clitoris. It's gone. I shouldn't have worn it swimming." The woman who ran the workshop laughed. She calmly stroked my forehead. She told me my clitoris was not something I could lose. It was me, the essence of me. It was both the doorbell to my house and the house itself. I didn't have to *find* it. I had to *be* it. Be it. Be my clitoris. Be my clitoris. I lay back and closed my eyes. I put the mirror down. I watched myself float above myself. I watched as I slowly began to approach myself and reenter. I felt like an astronaut reentering the atmosphere of the earth. It was very quiet, this re-entry: quiet and gentle. I bounced and landed, landed and bounced. I came into my own muscles and blood and cells and then I just slid into my vagina. It was suddenly easy and I fit. I was all warm and pulsing and ready and young and alive. And then, without looking, with my eyes still closed, I put my finger on what had suddenly become me. There was a little quivering at first, which urged me to stay. Then the quivering became a quake, an eruption, the layers dividing and subdividing. The quaking broke open into an ancient horizon of light and silence, which opened onto a plane of music and colors and innocence and longing, and I felt connection, calling connection as I lay there thrashing about on my little blue mat.

My vagina is a shell, a tulip, and a destiny. I am arriving as I am beginning to leave. My vagina, my vagina, me.

VAGINA FACT

"The clitoris is pure in purpose. It is the only organ in the body designed purely for pleasure. The clitoris is simply a bundle of nerves: 8,000 nerve fibers, to be precise. That's a higher concentration of nerve fibers than is found anywhere else in the body, including the fingertips, lips, and tongue, and it is twice . . . twice . . . twice the number in the penis. Who needs a handgun when you've got a semiautomatic."

—from *Woman: An Intimate Geography,* by Natalie Angier

BECAUSE HE LIKED TO LOOK AT IT

This is how I came to love my vagina. It's embarrassing, because it's not politically correct. I mean, I know it should have happened in a bath with salt grains from the Dead Sea, Enya playing, me loving my woman self. I know the story. Vaginas are beautiful. Our self-hatred is only the internalized repression and hatred of the patriarchal culture. It isn't real. Pussies unite. I know all of it. Like, if we'd grown up in a culture where we were taught that fat thighs were beautiful, we'd all be pounding down milkshakes and cookies, lying on our backs, spending our days thigh-expanding. But we didn't grow up in that culture. I hated my thighs, and I hated my vagina even more. I thought it was incredibly ugly. I was one of those women who had looked at it and, from that moment on, wished I hadn't. It made me sick. I pitied anyone who had to go down there.

In order to survive, I began to pretend there was something else between my legs. I imagined furniture—cozy futons with light cotton comforters, little velvet settees, leopard rugs—or pretty things—silk handkerchiefs, quilted pot holders, or place settings—or miniature landscapes—clear crystal lakes or moisty Irish bogs. I got so accustomed to this that I lost all memory of having a vagina. Whenever I had sex with a man, I pictured him inside a mink-lined muffler or a red rose or a Chinese bowl.

Then I met Bob. Bob was the most ordinary man I ever met. He was thin and tall and nondescript and wore khaki clothes. Bob did not like spicy foods or listen to Prodigy. He had no interest in sexy lingerie. In the summer he spent time in the shade. He did not share his inner feelings. He did not have any problems or issues, and was not even an alcoholic. He wasn't very funny or articulate or mysterious. He wasn't mean or unavailable. He wasn't self-involved or charismatic. He didn't drive fast. I didn't particularly like Bob. I would have missed him altogether if he hadn't picked up my change that I dropped on the deli floor. When he handed me back my quarters and pennies and his hand accidentally touched mine, something happened. I went to bed with him. That's when the miracle occurred.

Turned out that Bob loved vaginas. He was a connoisseur. He loved the way they felt, the way they tasted, the way they smelled, but most important, he loved the way they looked. He had to look at them. The first time we had sex, he told me he had to see me.

"I'm right here," I said.

“No, you,” he said. “I have to see you.”

“Turn on the light,” I said.

Thinking he was a weirdo, I was freaking out in the dark. He turned on the light.

Then he said, “Okay. I’m ready, ready to see you.”

“Right here.” I waved. “I’m right here.”

Then he began to undress me.

“What are you doing, Bob?” I said.

“I need to see you,” he replied.

“No need,” I said. “Just dive in.”

“I need to see what you look like,” he said.

“But you’ve seen a red leather couch before,” I said.

Bob continued. He would not stop. I wanted to throw up and die.

“This is awfully intimate,” I said. “Can’t you just dive in?”

“No,” he said. “It’s who you are. I need to look.”

I held my breath. He looked and looked. He gasped and smiled and stared and groaned. He got breathy and his face changed. He didn't look ordinary anymore. He looked like a hungry, beautiful beast.

"You're so beautiful," he said. "You're elegant and deep and innocent and wild."

"You saw that there?" I said.

It was like he read my palm.

"I saw that," he said, "and more—much, much more."

He stayed looking for almost an hour, as if he were studying a map, observing the moon, staring into my eyes, but it was my vagina. In the light, I watched him looking at me, and he was so genuinely excited, so peaceful and euphoric, I began to get wet and turned on. I began to see myself the way he saw me. I began to feel beautiful and delicious—like a great painting or a waterfall. Bob wasn't afraid. He wasn't grossed out. I began to swell, began to feel proud. Began to love my vagina. And Bob lost himself there and I was there with him, in my vagina, and we were gone.

MY VAGINA WAS MY VILLAGE

For the women of Bosnia

My vagina was green, water soft pink fields, cow mooing sun resting sweet boyfriend touching lightly with soft piece of blond straw.

There is something between my legs. I do not know what it is. I do not know where it is. I do not touch. Not now. Not anymore. Not since.

My vagina was chatty, can't wait, so much, so much saying, words talking, can't quit trying, can't quit saying, oh yes, oh yes.

Not since I dream there's a dead animal sewn in

down there with thick black fishing line. And the bad dead animal smell cannot be removed. And its throat is slit and it bleeds through all my summer dresses.

My vagina singing all girl songs, all goat bells ringing songs, all wild autumn field songs, vagina songs, vagina home songs.

Not since the soldiers put a long thick rifle inside me. So cold, the steel rod canceling my heart. Don't know whether they're going to fire it or shove it through my spinning brain. Six of them, monstrous doctors with black masks shoving bottles up me too. There were sticks, and the end of a broom.

My vagina swimming river water, clean spilling water over sun-baked stones over stone clit, clit stones over and over.

Not since I heard the skin tear and made lemon screeching sounds, not since a piece of my vagina came off in my hand, a part of the lip, now one side of the lip is completely gone.

My vagina. A live wet water village. My vagina my hometown.

Not since they took turns for seven days smelling

like feces and smoked meat, they left their dirty sperm inside me. I became a river of poison and pus and all the crops died, and the fish.

My vagina a live wet water village.
They invaded it. Butchered it and burned it down.
I do not touch now.
Do not visit.
I live someplace else now.
I don't know where that is.

VAGINA FACT

"In the nineteenth century, girls who learned to develop orgasmic capacity by masturbation were regarded as medical problems. Often they were 'treated' or 'corrected' by amputation or cautery of the clitoris or 'miniature chastity belts,' sewing the vaginal lips together to put the clitoris out of reach, and even castration by surgical removal of the ovaries. But there are no references in the medical literature to the surgical removal of testicles or amputation of the penis to stop masturbation in boys.

"In the United States, the last recorded clitoridectomy for curing masturbation was performed in 1948—on a five-year-old girl."

—*The Woman's Encyclopedia of Myths and Secrets*

VAGINA FACT

"Genital mutilation has been inflicted on [200 million] girls and young women. In countries where it is practiced, mostly African, [about 30 million young girls within the next decade] can expect the knife—or the razor or a glass shard—to cut their clitoris or remove it altogether, [and] to have part or all of the labia . . . sewn together with catgut or thorns.

"Often the operation is prettified as 'circumcision.' The African health specialist Nahid Toubia puts it plain: In a man it would range from amputation of most of the penis, to 'removal of all the penis, its roots of soft tissue and part of the scrotal skin.'

"Short-term results include tetanus, septicemia, hemorrhages, cuts in the urethra, bladder, vaginal walls, and anal sphincter. Long-term: chronic uterine infection, massive scars that can hinder walking for life, fistula formation, hugely increased agony and danger during childbirth, and early deaths."

—*The New York Times,* April 12, 1996, with updates (in brackets) from the 2013 UNICEF report "Female Genital Mutilation/Cutting: A Statistical Overview and Exploration of the Dynamics of Change"

MY ANGRY VAGINA

My vagina's angry. It is. It's pissed off. My vagina's furious and it needs to talk. It needs to talk about all this shit. It needs to talk to you. I mean, what's the deal? An army of people out there thinking up ways to torture my poor-ass, gentle, loving vagina. . . . Spending their days constructing psycho products and nasty ideas to undermine my pussy. Vagina motherfuckers.

All this shit they're constantly trying to

shove up us, clean us up—stuff us up, make it go away. Well, my vagina's not going away. It's pissed off and it's staying right here. Like tampons—what the hell is that? A wad of dry fucking cotton stuffed up there. Why can't they find a way to subtly lubricate the tampon? As soon as my vagina sees it, it goes into shock. It says, Forget it. It closes up. You need to work with the vagina, introduce it to things, prepare the way. That's what foreplay's all about. You got to convince my vagina, seduce my vagina, engage my vagina's trust. You can't do that with a dry wad of fucking cotton.

Stop shoving things up me. Stop shoving and stop cleaning it up. My vagina doesn't need to be cleaned up. It smells good already. Not like rose petals. Don't try to decorate. Don't believe him when he tells you it smells like rose petals when it's supposed to smell like pussy. That's what they're doing—trying to clean it up, make it smell like bathroom spray or a garden. All those douche sprays—floral, berry, rain. I don't want my pussy to smell like rain. All cleaned up like washing a fish after you cook it. Want to *taste* the fish. That's why I ordered it.

Then there's those exams. Who thought them up? There's got to be a better way to do those exams. Why the scary paper dress that scratches your tits and crunches when you lie down so you feel like a wad of paper someone threw away? Why the rubber gloves? Why the flashlight all up there like Nancy Drew working against gravity, why the Nazi steel stirrups, the mean cold duck lips they shove inside you? What's that? My vagina's angry about those visits. It gets defended weeks in advance. It shuts down, won't "relax." Don't you hate that? "Relax your vagina, relax your vagina." Why? My vagina's not stupid. Relax so you can shove those cold duck lips inside it? I don't think so.

Why can't they find some nice, delicious purple velvet and wrap it around me, lay me down on some feathery cotton spread, put on some nice, friendly pink or blue gloves, and rest my feet in some fur-covered stirrups? Warm up the duck lips. Work with my vagina.

But no, more tortures: dry wad of fucking cotton, cold duck lips, and thong underwear. That's the worst. Thong underwear. Who thought that up? Moves around all the time, gets stuck in the back of your vagina, real crusty butt.

Vagina's supposed to be loose and wide, not held together. That's why girdles are so bad. We need to move and spread and talk and talk. Vaginas need comfort. Make something like that, something to give them pleasure. No, of course they won't do that. Hate to see a woman having pleasure, particularly sexual pleasure. I mean, make a nice pair of soft cotton underwear with a French tickler built in. Women would be coming all day long, coming in the supermarket, coming on the subway, coming, happy vaginas. They wouldn't be able to stand it. Seeing all those energized, not-taking-shit, hot, happy vaginas.

If my vagina could talk, it would talk about itself like me; it would talk about other vaginas; it would do vagina impressions.

It would wear Harry Winston diamonds, no clothing—just there, all draped in diamonds.

My vagina helped release a giant baby. It thought it would be doing more of that. It's not. Now it wants to travel, doesn't want a lot of company. It wants to read and know things and get out more. It wants sex. It loves sex. It wants to go deeper. It's hungry for depth. It wants kindness. It wants change. It wants silence and freedom and gentle kisses and warm liquids and deep touch. It wants chocolate. It wants to scream. It wants to stop being angry. It wants to come. It wants to want. It wants. My vagina, my vagina. Well . . . it wants everything.

THE LITTLE COOCHI SNORCHER THAT COULD

[Southern woman]

Memory: December 1965; Five Years Old

My mama tells me in a scary, loud, life-threatening voice to stop scratching my coochi snorcher. I become terrified that I've scratched it off down there. I do not touch myself again, even in the bath. I am afraid of the water getting in and filling me up so I explode. I put Band-Aids over my coochi snorcher to cover the hole, but they fall off in the water. I imagine a stopper, a bathtub plug up there to prevent things from entering me. I sleep with three pairs of happy heart-patterned cotton underpants underneath my snap-up pajamas. I still want to touch myself, but I don't.

Memory: Seven Years Old

Edgar Montane, who is ten, gets angry at me and punches me with all his might between my legs. It feels like he breaks my entire self. I limp home. I can't pee. My mama asks me what's wrong with my coochi snorcher, and when I tell her what Edgar did to me she yells at me and says never to let anyone touch me down there again. I try to explain he didn't touch it, Mama, he punched it.

Memory: Nine Years Old

I play on the bed, bouncing and falling, and impale my coochi snorcher on the bedpost. I make high-pitched screamy noises that come straight from my coochi snorcher's mouth. I get taken to the hospital and they sew it up down there from where it's been torn apart.

Memory: Ten Years Old

I'm at my father's house and he's having a party upstairs. Everyone's drinking. I'm playing alone in the basement and I'm trying on my new white cotton bra and panties that my father's girlfriend gave me. Suddenly my father's best friend, this big man Alfred, comes up from behind and pulls my new underpants down and sticks his big hard penis into my coochi snorcher. I scream. I kick. I try to fight him off, but he already gets it in. My father's there then and he has a gun and there's a loud horrible noise and then there's blood all over Alfred and me, lots of blood. I'm sure my coochi snorcher is finally falling out. Alfred is paralyzed for life and my mama doesn't let me see my father for seven years.

Memory: Thirteen Years Old

My coochi snorcher is a very bad place, a place of pain, nastiness, punching, invasion, and blood. It's a site for mishaps. It's a bad-luck zone. I imagine a freeway between my legs and, girl, I am traveling, going far away from here.

Memory: Sixteen Years Old

There's this gorgeous twenty-four-year-old woman in our neighborhood and I stare at her all the time. One day she invites me into her car. She asks me if I like to kiss boys, and I tell her I do not like that. Then she says she wants to show me something, and she leans over and kisses me so softly on the lips with her lips and then puts her tongue in my mouth. Wow. She asks me if I want to come over to her house, and then she kisses me again and tells me to relax, to feel it, to let our tongues feel it. She asks my mama if I can spend the night and my mother's delighted that such a beautiful, successful woman has taken an interest in me. I'm scared but really I can't wait. Her apartment's fantastic. She's got it hooked up. It's the seventies: the beads, the fluffy pillows, the mood lights. I decide right there that I want to be a secretary like her when I grow up. She makes a vodka for herself and then she asks what I want to drink. I say the same as she's drinking and she says she doesn't think my mama would like me drinking vodka. I say she probably wouldn't like me kissing girls, either, and the pretty lady makes me a drink. Then she changes into this chocolate satin teddy. She's so beautiful. I always thought bulldaggers were ugly. I say, "You look great," and she says, "So do you." I say, "But I only have this white cotton bra and underpants." Then she dresses me, slowly, in another satin teddy. It's lavender like the first soft days of spring. The alcohol has gone to my head and I'm loose and ready. I noticed that there's a picture over her bed of a naked black woman with a huge afro as she gently and slowly lays me out on the bed. And just our bodies rubbing makes me come. Then she does everything to me and my coochi snorcher that I always thought was nasty before, and wow. I'm so hot, so wild. She says, "Your vagina, untouched by man, smells so nice, so fresh, wish I could keep it that way forever." I get crazy wild and then the phone rings and of course it's my mama. I'm sure she knows; she catches me at everything. I'm breathing so heavy and I try to act normal when

I get on the phone and she asks me, "What's wrong with you, have you been running?" I say, "No, Mama, exercising." Then she tells the beautiful secretary to make sure I'm not around boys and the lady tells her, "Trust me, there's no boys around here." Afterward the gorgeous lady teaches me everything about my coochi snorcher. She makes me play with myself in front of her and she teaches me all the different ways to give myself pleasure. She's very thorough. She tells me to always know how to give myself pleasure so I'll never need to rely on a man. In the morning I am worried that I've become a butch because I'm so in love with her. She laughs, but I never see her again. I realized later she was my surprising, unexpected, politically incorrect salvation. She transformed my sorry-ass coochi snorcher and raised it up into a kind of heaven.

"What does a vagina smell like?"

Earth.

Wet garbage.

God.

Water.

A brand-new morning.

Depth.

Sweet ginger.

Sweat.

Depends.

Musk.

Me.

No smell, I've been told.

Pineapple.

Chalice essence.

Paloma Picasso.

Earthy meat and musk.

Cinnamon and cloves.

Roses.

Spicy musky jasmine forest, deep, deep forest.

Damp moss.

Yummy candy.

The South Pacific.

Somewhere between fish and lilacs.

Peaches.

The woods.

Ripe fruit.

Strawberry-kiwi tea.

Fish.

Heaven.

Vinegar and water.

Light, sweet liquor.

Cheese.

Ocean.

Sexy.

A sponge.

The beginning.

RECLAIMING CUNT

I call it cunt. I've reclaimed it, "cunt." I really like it. "Cunt." Listen to it. "Cunt." C C, Ca Ca. Cavern, cackle, clit, cute, come—closed c—closed inside, inside ca—then u—then cu—then curvy, inviting sharkskin u—uniform, under, up, urge, ugh, ugh, u—then n then cun—snug letters fitting perfectly together—n—nest, now, nexus, nice, nice, always depth, always round in uppercase, cun, cun—n a jagged wicked electrical pulse—n [*high-pitched noise*] then soft n—warm n—cun, cun, then t—then sharp certain tangy t—texture, take, tent, tight, tantalizing, tensing, taste, tendrils, time, tactile, tell me, tell me "Cunt cunt," say it, tell me "Cunt." "Cunt."

I ASKED A SIX-YEAR-OLD GIRL:

"If your vagina got dressed, what would it wear?"

"Red high-tops and a Mets cap worn backward."

"If it could speak, what would it say?"

"It would say words that begin with 'V' and 'T'—'turtle' and 'violin' are examples."

"What does your vagina remind you of?"

"A pretty dark peach. Or a diamond I found from a treasure and it's mine."

"What's special about your vagina?"

"Somewhere deep inside it I know it has a really really smart brain."

"What does your vagina smell like?"

"Snowflakes."

THE WOMAN WHO LOVED TO MAKE VAGINAS HAPPY

I love vaginas. I love women. I do not see them as separate things. Women pay me to dominate them, to excite them, to make them come. I did not start out like this. No, to the contrary: I started out as a lawyer. But in my late thirties, I became obsessed with making women happy. There were so many unfulfilled women. So many women who had no access to their sexual happiness. It began as a mission of sorts, but then I got involved in it. I got very good at it, kind of brilliant. It was my art. I started getting paid for it. It was as if I had found my calling. Tax law seemed completely boring and insignificant then.

I wore outrageous outfits when I dominated women—lace and silk and leather—and I used props: whips, handcuffs, rope, dildos. There was nothing like this in tax law. There were no props, no excitement, and I hated those blue corporate suits, although I wear them now from time to time in my new line of work and they serve quite nicely. Context is all. There were no props, no outfits in corporate law. There was no wetness. There was no dark mysterious foreplay. There were no erect nipples. There were no delicious mouths, but mainly there was no moaning. Not the kind I'm talking about, anyway. This was the key, I see now; moaning was the thing that ultimately seduced me and got me addicted to making women happy. When I was a little girl and I would see women in the movies making love, making strange orgasmic moaning noises, I used to laugh. I got strangely hysterical. I couldn't believe that big, outrageous, ungoverned sounds like that just came out of women.

I longed to moan. I practiced in front of my mirror, on a tape recorder, moaning in various keys, various tones, with sometimes very operatic expressions, sometimes with more reserved, almost withheld expressions. But always when I played it back, it sounded fake. It *was* fake. It wasn't rooted in anything sexual, really, only in my desire to be sexual.

But then when I was ten I had to pee really badly once. On a car trip. It went on for almost an hour and when I finally got to pee in this dirty little gas station, it was so exciting, I moaned. I moaned as I peed. I couldn't believe it, me moaning in a Texaco station somewhere in the middle of Louisiana. I realized right then that moans are connected with not getting what you want right away, with putting things off. I realized moans were best when they caught you by surprise; they came out of this hidden mysterious part of you that was speaking its own language. I realized that moans were, in fact, that language.

I became a moaner. It made most men anxious. Frankly, it terrified them. I was loud and they couldn't concentrate on what they were doing. They'd lose focus. Then they'd lose everything. We couldn't make love in people's homes. The walls were too thin. I got a reputation in my building, and people stared at me with contempt in the elevator. Men thought I was too intense; some called me insane.

I began to feel bad about moaning. I got quiet and polite. I made noise into a pillow. I learned to choke my moan, hold it back like a sneeze. I began to get headaches and stress-related disorders. I was becoming hopeless when I discovered women. I discovered that most women loved my moaning—but, more important, I discovered how deeply excited I got when other women moaned, when I could make other women moan. It became a kind of passion.

Discovering the key, unlocking the vagina's mouth, unlocking this voice, this wild song.

I made love to quiet women and I found this place inside them and they shocked themselves in their moaning. I made love to moaners and they found a deeper, more penetrating moan. I became obsessed. I longed to make women moan, to be in charge, like a conductor, maybe, or a bandleader.

It was a kind of surgery, a kind of delicate science, finding the tempo, the exact location or home of the moan. That's what I called it.

Sometimes I found it over a woman's jeans. Sometimes I sneaked up on it, off the record, quietly disarming the surrounding alarms and moving in. Sometimes I used force, but not violent, oppressing force, more like dominating, "I'm going to take you someplace; don't worry, lie back, enjoy the ride" kind of force. Sometimes it was simply mundane. I found the moan before things even started, while we were eating salad or chicken just casually right there, with my fingers,

"Here it is like that," real simple, in the kitchen, all mixed in with the balsamic vinegar. Sometimes I used props—I loved props—sometimes I made the woman find her own moan in front of me. I waited, stuck it out until she opened herself. I wasn't fooled by the minor, more obvious moans. No, I pushed her further, all the way into her power moan.

There's the clit moan (a soft, in-the-mouth sound), the vaginal moan (a deep, in-the-throat sound), the combo clit-vaginal moan. There's the pre-moan (a hint of sound), the almost moan (a circling sound), the right-on-it moan (a deeper, definite sound), the elegant moan (a sophisticated laughing sound), the Grace Slick moan (a rock-singing sound), the WASP moan (no sound), the semireligious moan (a Muslim chanting sound), the mountaintop moan (a yodeling sound), the baby moan (a googie-googie-googie-goo sound), the doggy moan (a panting sound), the southern moan (southern accent—"yeah! yeah"), the uninhibited militant bisexual moan (a deep, aggressive, pounding sound), the machine-gun moan, the tortured Zen moan (a twisted, hungry sound), the diva moan (a high, operatic note), the twisted-toe-orgasm moan, and, finally, the surprise triple orgasm moan.

I WAS THERE IN THE ROOM

For Shiva and Coco

I was there when her vagina opened.
We were all there: her mother, her husband,
    and I,
and the nurse from the Ukraine with her
    whole hand
up there in her vagina feeling and turning with
    her rubber
glove as she talked casually to us—like she was
    turning on a loaded faucet.

I was there in the room when the contractions
made her crawl on all fours,
made unfamiliar moans leak out of her pores
and still there after hours when she just
screamed suddenly
wild, her arms striking at the electric air.

I was there when her vagina changed
from a shy sexual hole
to an archaeological tunnel, a sacred vessel,
a Venetian canal, a deep well with a tiny stuck
child inside,
waiting to be rescued.

I saw the colors of her vagina. They changed.
Saw the bruised broken blue
the blistering tomato red
the gray pink, the dark;
saw the blood like perspiration along the edges
saw the yellow, white liquid, the shit, the clots
pushing out all the holes, pushing harder and
harder,

saw through the hole, the baby's head
scratches of black hair, saw it just there behind
the bone—a hard round memory,
as the nurse from the Ukraine kept turning and
turning
her slippery hand.

I was there when each of us, her mother and I,
held a leg and spread her wide pushing
with all our strength against her pushing
and her husband sternly counting, "One, two,
three,"
telling her to focus, harder.
We looked into her then.
We couldn't get our eyes out of that place.

We forget the vagina, all of us.
What else would explain
our lack of awe, our lack of wonder?

I was there when the doctor
reached in with Alice in Wonderland spoons

and there as her vagina became a wide operatic
mouth
singing with all its strength;
first the little head, then the gray flopping arm,
then the fast
swimming body, swimming quickly into our
weeping arms.

I was there later when I just turned and faced
her vagina.
I stood and let myself see
her all spread, completely exposed,
mutilated, swollen, and torn,
bleeding all over the doctor's hands
who was calmly sewing her there.

I stood, and as I stared, her vagina suddenly
became a wide red pulsing heart.

The heart is capable of sacrifice.
So is the vagina.
The heart is able to forgive and repair.

It can change its shape to let us in.
It can expand to let us out.
So can the vagina.
It can ache for us and stretch for us, die for us
and bleed and bleed us into this difficult,
    wondrous world.
So can the vagina.
I was there in the room.
I remember.

SPOTLIGHT MONOLOGUES

Each of these monologues was written for a V-Day Spotlight or a situation in the world where women were totally at risk, where they had been raped or murdered or dismissed or simply not allowed to be. It was my honor to be invited into these communities. It is my hope that in the telling of these stories where women suffered, they will be healed; that in seeing what erased them, they will be made forever visible, honored, and protected.

THE MEMORY OF HER FACE

For Esther

Islamabad

They all knew something terrible
Was going to happen
Each time he came home
The things he used
First time
He grabbed the closest thing
He grabbed a pot
He smashed her head

E
V
E

E
N
S
L
E
R

He smashed her right eye hard
The next time
He thought about it a little
And paused
Took off his belt
She had gashes inside her thighs
The third time he needed to be more
Involved in hurting her
So he beat her with his fists
He broke her nose
They heard her screams
They heard her beg
They didn't, wouldn't intervene
She was his
Unwritten law.
Don't ask what she had done
It was just her face that pissed him off
Just her needy face waiting for more
The last time he
Had enough of her
He planned it out
He got the acid in advance

He poured it in a jar
She said she needed money for food for
  them
She looked like that.
Like that. Like that. Like that.
Her face is gone
Totally melted off
Just eyes that's all you see
That's all
Just eyes encased in gooey flesh
I tell you this because
She's there inside this mess
Inside this monstrous mask
Inside the death of her esteem
Inside his wish to make her none
She's there, I swear
I heard her wheeze
I heard her sigh
I heard her babble something
With what was once her mouth
I heard her. I swear
She lives in there.

Juárez

Each woman is dark, particular, young
Each woman has brown eyes
Each woman is gone
There is one girl missing for ten months
She was seventeen when they took her away
She worked in the maquiladora
She stamped thousands of coupons for products
She would never afford
Four dollars a day
They paid her and bused her to the desert
To sleep in freezing shit
It must have been on the way to the bus
They took her
It must have been dark outside
It must have lasted until morning
Whatever they did to her
It went on and on
You can tell from the others
Who showed up without hands or nipples
It must have gone on and on
When she finally reappeared

She was bone
Bone bone
No cute mole above her right eye
No naughty smile, no wavy black hair
Bone she came back as bone
She and the others
All beautiful
All beginning
All coupons
All faces
All gone
300 faces gone
300 noses
300 chins
300 dark penetrating eyes
300 smiles
300 mulatto cheeks
300 hungry mouths
about to speak
about to tell
about to scream
gone now bone.

I tried to turn away
When she lifted her chador
in the restaurant
When they raised the plastic cloth
that concealed
the bone outline of her head
in the morgue
I tried to turn away.

UNDER THE BURQA

For Zoya

(This piece is not about the burqa per se. Wearing one is obviously a matter of culture and choice. The piece is about a time and place where women had no choice.)

imagine a huge dark piece of cloth
hung over your entire body
like you were a shameful statue
imagine there's only a drop of light
enough to know there is still daylight for others
imagine it's hot, very hot
imagine you are being encased in cloth,

drowning in fabric, in darkness
imagine you are begging in this bedspread
reaching out your hand inside the cloth
which must remain covered, unpolished, unseen
or they might smash it or cut it off
imagine no one is putting rubies in your
    invisible hand
because no one can see your face
so you do not exist
imagine you cannot find your children
because they came for your husband
the only man you ever loved
even though it was an arranged marriage
because they came and shot him with the gun
of his they could not find
and you tried to defend him and they
    trampled you
four men on your back
in front of your screaming children
imagine you went mad
but you did not know you were mad
because you were living under a bedspread

and you hadn't seen the sun in years
and you lost your way
and you remembered your two daughters
vaguely
like a dream the way you remembered sky
imagine muttering as a way of talking
because words did not form anymore in the
darkness
and you did not cry because it got too hot and
wet in there
imagine bearded men that you could only
decipher
by their smell
checking your socks and beating you
because they were white
imagine being flogged
in front of people you could not see
imagine being humiliated so deeply
that there was no face attached to it
and no air. it got darker there
imagine no peripheral vision
so like a wounded animal

you could not defend yourself
or even duck from the sideward blows
imagine that laughter was banned
throughout your country and music
and the only sounds you heard
were the muffled sounds of the azun
or the cries of other women flogged
inside their cloth, inside their dark
imagine you could no longer distinguish
between living and dying
so you stopped trying to kill yourself
because it would be redundant
imagine you had no place to live
your roof was the cloth
as you wandered the streets
and this tomb
was getting smaller and smellier every day
you were beginning to walk into things
imagine suffocating while you were still
    breathing
imagine muttering and screaming
inside a cage

and no one is hearing
imagine me inside the inside
of the darkness in you
i am caught there
i am lost there
inside the cloth
which is your head
inside the dark we share
imagine you can see me
i was beautiful once
big dark eyes
you would know me

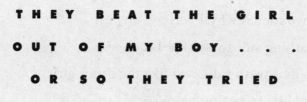

THEY BEAT THE GIRL OUT OF MY BOY . . . OR SO THEY TRIED

For Calpernia and Andrea

At five years old
I was putting my baby sister's
diapers on
I saw her vagina
I wanted one
I wanted one
I thought it would grow
I thought I would open
I ached to belong

I ached to smell
like my mother
Her aroma lived in my hair
on my hands, in my skin
I ached to be pretty
Pretty
I wondered why I was missing my
bathing suit top at the beach
Why I wasn't dressed like the other girls
I ached to be completed
I ached to belong
To spin the baton
They assigned me a sex
The day I was born
It's as random as being adopted
or being assigned a hotel room on the thirtieth
floor
It has nothing to do with who you are
or your fear of heights.
But in spite of the apparatus
I was forced to carry around
I always knew I was a girl

They beat me for it
They beat me for crying
They pummeled me for wanting
To touch
To pet
To hug
To help
To hold
Their hands
For trying to fly in church
like Sister Bertrille
For doing cartwheels
Crocheting socks
For carrying purses to kindergarten
They kicked the shit out of me every day
on my way to school.
In the park
they smashed my
Magic Marker painted nails
They punched my lipsticked mouth
They beat the girl
out of my boy

or they tried
So I went underground
I stopped playing the flute
"Be a man, stand up for yourself
Go punch him back."
I grew a full beard
It was good I was big
I joined the Marines
"Suck it up and drive on."
I became duller
Jaded
Sometimes cruel
Butch it
Butch it
Butch it up
Always clenched, inaccurate,
Incomplete
I ran away from home
from school
from boot camp.
Ran to Miami
Greenwich Village

The Aleutian Islands
New Orleans
I found gay people
Wilderness lesbians
Got my first hormone shot
Got permission to be myself
To transition
To travel
To immigrate
350 hours of hot needles
I would count the male particles as they died
Sixteen man hairs gone
The feminine is in your face
I lift my eyebrows more
I'm curious
I ask questions.
And my voice
Practice practice
It's all about resonance
Sing song sing song
Men are monotone and flat
Southern accents are really excellent

Jewish accents really help.
"Hello my friend"
And my vagina is so much friendlier
I cherish it
It brings me joy
The orgasms come in waves
Before they were jerky
I'm the girl next door
My Lieutenant Colonel father ended
up paying for it
My vagina
My mother was worried
what people would think
of her, that she made this happen
until I came to church
and everyone said you have a beautiful
daughter
I wanted to belong
I got to be soft
I am allowed to listen
I am allowed to touch
I am able to receive.

To be in the present tense
People are so much nicer to me now
I can wake up in the morning
Put my hair in a ponytail
A wrong was righted
I am right with God
It's like when you're trying to sleep
And there is a loud car alarm
When I got my vagina, it was like someone
Finally turned it off
I live now in the female zone
But you know how people feel about immigrants
They don't like it when you come from
someplace else
They don't like it when you mix
They killed my boyfriend
They beat him insanely as he slept
With a baseball bat
They beat this girl
Out of his head
They didn't want him
Dating a foreigner

Even though she was pretty
And she listened and was kind
They didn't want him falling in love
with ambiguity.
They were that terrified of love.

(This piece was based on interviews with transgender women from all over America.)

CROOKED BRAID

For the women from the Oglala Lakota Nation

1

He wanted to go out.
He said to me "You stay home"
I said "I wanted to go out"
He said "You have a baby"
I said "It's our baby"
I laid the baby down.
He probably felt my tension
because he was whimpering,

the baby.
I looked up
and he slapped me, my husband.
Not a blast that knocks your eyes blue.
That came later.
It was a smack,
a hard domestic smack.
He looked at me.
He was smiling.
I couldn't believe it.
He was smiling.
He slapped me again.
His dad was vicious to his mother.
I saw him smile.
What was that?
He was the nicest person.
He had long black hair.
When we made love it got
loose
before.

2

He took me to the dinner,
made me go out with his boss.
I didn't want to go.
He kicked me under the table,
told me to look happy,
told me to smile.
I smiled.
He kicked me again,
asked me who I was trying to
fuck, told me to stop coming
on to everyone.
I stopped smiling.
He kicked me again.
This went on and on.
Outside the restaurant
he grabbed my hair
and pulled me down to
the curb.
It had been snowing.
He buried me in snow.
He pounded me in the gutter.

The snow was melting.
It was sloppy.
My hair felt like it was bleeding.

3

He was drinking.
I was too.
I must have blacked out.
I woke up in the hospital
after five brain surgeries.
My hair was gone.
They shaved it off.
I had to relearn to talk
and move my arms.
It took me four months
to remember how to cook
breakfast.
I remember putting
the egg in the frying pan
with the bacon.
I knew the egg felt right
I just didn't remember to

crack it open.
Just the egg in the frying pan
in its shell.
My head was bald.

4

Eighteen years
he beat me.
In the morning
when he was so nice again
I would braid his long hair.
I would take my time
like I cared so much
and I would do it perfectly crooked.
I would make the hairs
so they would stand up
all crazy like.
Then he'd go forgetting
that the bruises on my
face were his handprints.
He'd walk all cocky in the street.
All macho in the road,

but his braid would be so crooked
and look so stupid and wrong.
This shouldn't have made me that happy.
It really just shouldn't have made me that happy.

5

Heard that he was out
with a woman
making love and she was fluffing
his hair when he was wild
on top of her.
He came home
much later
and his hair was braided up all
right and tight.
He passed out
from drinking.
Then I got up
with scissors
as he snored
and slowly walked to him
and just cut the braid off,

completely off,
and put it in his hand
so that when he woke
up he screamed
"What the
fuck? I am going to kill you"
and he jumped up,
but I had tied his shoes together
so he couldn't run.
I didn't go
back to him for three years
until I knew his hair had grown out again.

6

I didn't want to have sex with him.
He was drunk.
I was just a piece of meat
to him,
a hole.
I tried to pretend
I was asleep.
He elbowed me, jerked me

pulled me up.
I remember thinking just get it over with.
He was soft and kept pumping
and pumping until
I got sore.
I said "It didn't feel good."
He said "Who were you with?
Was he bigger than
me? Did you like it?"
You're like a mouse with a lion.
You have to move fast
to the door.
He picked me up
like I was a rag.
His eyes were numb.
I could hear my son screaming,
his mouth was open and
his tonsils,
I could see his tonsils.
My husband beat the shit out of me.
He wrapped my long black hair around his hand,
jerked my head.

I tried to get my son.
"That's not your son," he said,
holding my hair in his hand.
"That's not your son anymore."

Now he calls me the middle
of night
weeping.
He didn't mean to beat his wife.
He didn't mean to batter her.
He's suicidal.
He knows what his mother went through.
But he can't stop—my son.
They took our land.
They took our ways.
They took our men.
We want them back.

(This piece was based on interviews with Indigenous women on the Pine Ridge Reservation.)

SAY IT

For the "Comfort Women"

Our stories only exist inside our heads
Inside our ravaged bodies
Inside a time and space of war
And emptiness
There is no paper trail
Nothing official on the books
Only conscience
Only this
What we were promised:

That I would save my father if I went with
  them
That I would find a job
That I would serve the country
That they would kill me if I didn't go
That it was better there
What we found:
No mountains
No trees
No water
Yellow sand
A desert
A warehouse full of tears
Thousands of worried girls
My braid cut against my will
No time to wear panties
What we were forced to do:
Change our names
Wear one-piece dresses with
A button that opened easily
Fifty Japanese soldiers a day
Sometimes there would be a ship of them

Strange barbaric things
Do it even when we bleed
Do it young before we started bleeding
There were so many
Some wouldn't take off their clothes
Just took out their penis
So many men I couldn't walk
I couldn't stretch my legs
I couldn't bend
I couldn't
What they did to us over and over:
Cursed
Spanked
Twisted
Tore bloody inside out
Sterilized
Drugged
Slapped
Punched
What we saw:
A girl drinking chemicals in the bathroom
A girl killed by a bomb

A girl beaten with a rifle over and over
A girl running headfirst into a wall
A girl's malnourished body dumped in the river
To drown
What we weren't allowed to do:
Wash ourselves
Move around
Go to the doctor
Use a condom
Run away
Keep my baby
Ask him to stop
What we caught:
Malaria
Syphilis
Gonorrhea
Stillbirths
Tuberculosis
Heart disease
Nervous breakdowns
Hypochondria
What we were fed:

Rice
Miso soup
Turnip pickle
Rice
Miso soup
Turnip pickle
Rice rice rice
What we became:
Ruined
Tools
Infertile
Holes
Bloody
Meat
Exiled
Silenced
Alone
What we were left with:
Nothing
A shocked father who never recovered
And died
No wages

Scars

Hatred of men

No children

No house

A space where a uterus once was

Booze

Smoking

Guilt

Shame

What we got called:

Ianfu—Comfort Women

Shugyofu—Women of Indecent Occupation

What we felt:

My chest still trembles

What got taken:

The springtime

My life

What we are:

74

79

84

93

Blind
Slow
Ready
Outside the Japanese Embassy every Wednesday
No longer afraid
What we want:
Now soon
Before we're gone
And our stories leave this world,
Leave our heads
Japanese government
Say it
Please
We are sorry, Comfort Women
Say it to me
We are sorry to me
We are sorry to me
To me
To me
To me
Say it.
Say sorry

Say we are sorry

Say me

See me

Say it

Sorry.

(This piece was based on the testimonies of the Comfort Women.)

FOR MY SISTERS IN PORTAUPRINCEBUKA-VUNEWORLEANS

what broken earthquaked bombed
out worn down worn over levee flooded what
    bright yellow green

speckled mango sitting dust light barefooted pig

walking goat crossing garbage piled high cement
    broken hot daylight hungry history
    shackled hands missing rubber

cutting boy running girl bleeding displaced
evacuee

exiled water coming earth cracking houses falling

U.S. guards guns pointing what red yellow green
X no body markings what cold company
men buying warm dead-bodied land out
from under

what money promised nine billion twenty-nine
billion many billion

never arriving billion what x presidents missing

presidents corrupt presidents what four-year-old
six-year-old eighteen-year-old raped

open
insuperdomecampburningvillage

what outside well-intended saving and rendering
powerless

victims made victims victims what melting
penetrable tents

skin soul what world what people having
everything

keep going while garbage swallows boys digging

children sinking

what women carrying charcoal sacks

potatoes sacks carrying mini knives mace under
bright

colored pagne skirts carrying babies on breasts
backs

carrying songs dances churches fields hurt
centers

carrying possibility bellies beings words what
women carrying

on outshining filth outshining odds what
happens now

New Orleans Haiti Congo women now

or never women claiming what they carry
claiming carrying now

women colored brightly carrying everything
everything carrying on . . .

Myriam Merlet was an activist and an author. She was chief of staff of the Ministry for Gender and the Rights of Women of Haiti and the founder of ENFOFANM, which collects and promotes women's stories and fights for women's rights through the media. She was extraordinary and beloved and brought V-Day and The Vagina Monologues *to Haiti.*

She died in the earthquake of 2010.

MYRIAM

Myriam,
Almost a year has passed
since I began calling you
calling and calling
believing the ring
would find you and wake you
your cell still gripped in your buried hand.

A year since
those days of exploding

living rooms and limbs
the blizzard of cement and bone.

Those days of body bags
and not enough body bags
of silent babies wandering the remains
and mad digging
and sometimes screams or sometimes prayers.

Those days right after
Haiti collapsed
like a house of stars
you who had been holding it up
now, suddenly under it.

Myriam,
There are women
in the streets, in cars
in camps, in ragged patchwork tents
women hardly clothed
grabbed by hungry angry men
filled with babies not their own

there are women who
in order to work
must leave
their daughters
women with blood on their legs
terrified to take a bath.
Here are women waiting to sleep
waiting for doors and roofs and walls
or
there are women refusing to wait
women calling up your memory
your name:

You worked hard to change all this
like the biblical prophetess
returned to your land
tambourine in hand
to sing the stories of your women.
You knew the future of Haiti depended on it.

You and Magalie and Anne Marie and all the
others

who broke down the gates
who changed the street names, packed the
courtrooms, made new laws.
Your bodies may be lying
amidst the steel and dust
but you did not perish there
we are not giving up
we are singing your song
emboldened by your name
Myriam Merlet.
Myriam, Myriam.

HEY MISS PAT

For Patricia Henry
and for the Katrina Warriors of New Orleans and the Gulf South

They come to my gate
They holler at me:
"Hey Miss Pat
Whatcha cooking?"
They do it every day.
They know I can't cook a little.
I cook for everyone. I cook a lot.

Just now it was the mother of that big boy
Who caught asthma in the trailer

From all that FEMAldehyde.
Those trailers weren't meant for more
Than twenty minutes
And they certainly can't hold no big people.
Poor woman, she worried worried tired.
I cooked her up some fried fish and some dirty
rice.

New Orleans ain't what it was.
Used to be bingo
Used to be Walmarts open 24/7
You could shop at midnight or one A.M.
Used to have lay ways
Every time you got your little money
You could pay some things off
Now no one's saving up for any future.

"Hey Miss Pat
Whatcha cooking?"
They found her mama dead last week
Only twenty-nine
They said she died of complications

But that's what they say now
When someone kills themselves
Her poor mother was never right after the
flood
I heard she drank cleaning fluid.

If I wasn't born here, I swear I would pick up
and leave
My daughter is a single parent
The more she works the less she has
She can't pay the bills
And buy the class ring for her daughter
Or a gown for the prom
I be feeling bad
But I push it aside.

"Hey Miss Pat
Whatcha cooking?"
That's my best friend Mary.
She helps me cook sometimes
I think it keeps her mind off things
We're making sandwiches today for

The folks walking past in the second line
They're killing my friend Mary
Trying to run her out of here
They call it fuel adjustment. They charge her so
much a month. But she doesn't have gas.
They took the gas meter out.

My husband is in construction
He doesn't get work much now
It's the rain or all the men they brought in
cheap
From out of town.
He holds up this ragged sign all day and sells
pecans,
A dollar a bag
It's made him someone else
It took away his man

Most taxi drivers won't bring folks to our street
They say they could get shot or killed
So I wonder what that makes me
A person who is bulletproof or already dead.

"Hey Miss Pat
Whatcha cooking?"
It's my pastor
He wants yakamein soup
Noodles green onions beef soy sauce and eggs
His wife don't know how to make it
And she surely won't learn
I like my pastor happy and full
He preaches stronger

We fixed the roof of our little church
We fixed the floors
My pastor says we are going to make it
 through
He says this will make us better than before.

"Hey Miss Pat
Whatcha cooking?"
I hear her calling me sometimes
Whispering crazy at my door
Miss Ruby who was eighty-two and ate up all
 my barbecued shrimp

I didn't mind 'cause she was rail-thin
She didn't want to go noplace else
Stayed too long up on her roof
The water took her away
But she's here
Like the others
Whispering at my gate
Hey Miss Pat
Miss Pat
I'm hungry
I'm trying to get home.

You holler for me at the gate, okay
I'll get you something to eat
I'm cooking up a remedy
I'm cooking up some serious rage
I'm cooking up a levee that will hold
And a government that will care
I'm adding water and salt and
A pinch of defiance
I'm cooking up sorrow
And family

I'm cooking up gumbo okra jambalaya mac and
cheese roast beef and resistance
I'm cooking up spices and ancestors
And a right and a way to stay in this place
I'm cooking
Oh I'm cooking
I'm cooking.

OVER IT

I am over rape.
I am over rape happening in broad daylight.
I am over rape culture, rape mentality.
I am over rape pages on Facebook.
I am over the thousands of people who signed
those pages with their real names without
shame.

E V E E N S L E R

I am over people demanding their right to rape pages, and calling it freedom of speech or justifying it as a joke.
I am over being told I don't have a sense of humor, and women don't have a sense of humor, when most women I know are really fucking funny. We just don't think that uninvited penises up our anus or our vagina is a laugh riot.

I am over how long it seems to take anyone to ever respond to rape.
I am over the hundreds of thousands of women in Congo still waiting for the rapes to end and the rapists to be held accountable.
I am over the thousands of women in Bosnia, Burma, Pakistan, South Africa, Guatemala, Sierra Leone, Haiti, Afghanistan, Libya, you name a place, still waiting for justice.

I am over rape happening in broad daylight.
I am over the rape clinics in Ecuador that

captured, raped, and tortured lesbians to make them straight.

I am over one in three women in the U.S. military getting raped by their so-called "comrades."

I am over the forces that deny women who have been raped the right to have an abortion.

I am over the fraternity boys at University of Vermont voting on who they would most like to rape.

I am over rape victims becoming re-raped when they go public.

I am over starving Somali women being raped at the Dadaab refugee camp in Kenya, and I am over women getting raped at Occupy Wall Street and being quiet about it because they were protecting a movement that is fighting to end the pillaging and raping of the economy and the earth, as if the rape of their bodies was something separate.

I am over women still being silent about rape because they are made to believe it's their fault.

I am over violence against women not being an international priority when one out of three women will be raped or beaten in her lifetime—the destruction and muting and undermining of women is the destruction of life itself.

No women, no future, duh.

I am over this rape culture where the privileged with political and physical and economic might take what and who they want, when they want it, as much as they want, anytime they want it.

I am over the endless resurrection of the careers of rapists and sexual exploiters—film directors, world leaders, corporate executives, movie stars, athletes—while the lives of those they violated are permanently destroyed, often forcing women to live in social and emotional exile.

I am over the passivity of good men. Where the hell are you?

You live with us, make love with us, father us, befriend us, brother us, get nurtured and mothered and eternally supported by us, so why aren't you standing with us? Why aren't you driven to madness and action by the rape and humiliation of us?

I am over years and years of being over rape

and thinking about rape every day of my life since I was five years old

and getting sick from rape, and depressed from
rape, and enraged by rape
and reading my insanely crowded inbox of rape
horror stories every hour of every single
day.

I am over being polite about rape. It's been too
long now, we have been too understanding.

We need people to truly try and imagine—once
and for all—what it feels like to have your
body invaded, your mind splintered, your
soul shattered.
We need to OCCUPYRAPE in every school,
park, radio, TV station, household, office,
factory, refugee camp, military base, back
room, nightclub, alleyway, courtroom, UN
office.

Because we are over it.

MY REVOLUTION BEGINS IN THE BODY

For the women in Tondo, Philippines

My revolution begins in the body
It isn't waiting anymore
My revolution does not need approval or
permission
It happens because it has to happen in each
neighborhood, village, city, or town
At gatherings of tribes, fellow students, women
at the market, on the bus
It may be gradual and soft

It may be spontaneous and loud
It may be happening already
It may be found in your closet, your drawers,
 your gut, your legs, your multiplying cells
In the naked mouth of taut nipples and
 overflowing breasts
My revolution is swelling from the insatiable
 drumming between my legs
My revolution is willing to die for this
My revolution is ready to live big
My revolution is overthrowing the state
Of mind called patriarchy
My revolution will not be choreographed
Although it begins with a few familiar steps
My revolution is not violent but it does not shy
 away from the dangerous edges where fierce
 displays of resistance tumble into
 something new

My revolution is in this body
In these hips gripped by misogyny
In this jaw wired mute by hunger and atrocity

My revolution is
Connection not consumption
Passion not profit
Orgasm not ownership
My revolution is of the earth and will come from
her
For her, because of her
It understands that every time we frack or drill
Or burn or violate the layers of her sacredness
We violate the soul of our future
My revolution is not ashamed to press my body
down
On her mud floor in front
Banyan, cypress, pine, Kalayaan, oak, chestnut,
mulberry
Redwood, sycamore trees
To bow shamelessly to shocking yellow birds and
rose-blue setting skies, heart exploding
purple bougainvillea and aqua sea
My revolution gladly kisses the feet of mothers
and nurses and servers and cleaners and
nannies

And healers and all who are life and give life
My revolution is on its knees
On my knees to every holy thing
And to those who carry empire-made burdens
In and on their heads and backs and
Hearts
My revolution demands abandon
Expects the original
Relies on troublemakers, anarchists, poets,
    shamans, seers, sexual explorers
Mystic travelers, tightrope walkers, and those
    who go too far and feel
Too much
My revolution shows up unexpectedly
It's not naïve but believes in miracles
Cannot be categorized targeted branded
Or even located
Offers prophecy not prescription
Is determined by mystery and ecstatic joy
Requires listening
Is not centralized though we all know where
    we're going

It happens in stages and all at once
It happens where you live and everywhere
It understands that divisions are diversions
It requires sitting still and staring deep into my
eyes
Go ahead
Love.

THEN WE WERE JUMPING

In the dream he comes
And sits across from me
At something that looks like a table
But has a constellation of stars
painted on the top of it
He is wearing his old yellow sweater
That he used to wear only in the house
And he looks uneasy
Older than I remember

And sad
Really sad
I remember this sadness
I lived in this sadness
Like a fog
Like a virus
I gave my body to him
To make the sadness go away
He took my body to make the sadness less
And when that didn't work
He made me as sad as him.

But here now at the table with the stars
And the falling galaxy that seems to
Come alive between us
I know surely that his sadness belongs to him
And I don't move
Away or toward
I feel strangely confident
I look up and realize
There is a vast circle
Of thousands maybe millions

Of people sitting around us
And we are in something like
a coliseum
and people are patient and quietly waiting
some women are knitting pot holders and others
red flags
a few men are leaning forward in their seats
smoking cigarettes
some are wearing strange hats
almost like they are clowns
they are not the kind of people
my father would have talked to
and they know this
but they are not unkind
my father suddenly gets annoyed
angry the way he used to get really
angry impatient and he says with a mean face,
"What are you looking for?"
He seems so small so fragile
I know I am not meant to save him
And then this silence
descends

a jar of liquid
light
around us
holding us, containing us
and out of nowhere
this clot, this dirty bloody transparent clot
filled with sharp noises and scraps of cruelty
    (fists, scissors, razor blades, words like
    "idiot," "hate," "you'll never . . . ," etc.)
starts coming out of me
out of all the parts of my body
pouring out of me
gathering
into one huge clot
and it floats like a murky rain cloud
hovering over my father's head
like it is expecting something
and my father takes a beat
looks up
and then he just opens his mouth
so natural, so easy
and receives my river of

pain, he swallows it whole
and all the people start cheering
wildly cheering and singing
and dancing
I can't take my eyes off him
My father becomes so full
his cheeks bulging and red
almost about to explode
not able to take much more
and then these red tears begin to
pour down my father's cheeks
I'm a little scared—it looks like he's crying blood
But the people are still cheering
They are so encouraging
This goes on for a while
My father crying and crying blood-red tears
And as I am looking because I won't stop
    looking at him
My father suddenly becomes a boy
and he isn't sad
he is dazzling and clever and playful
he takes me by the hand

and walks me out into the center
of the coliseum, which is
now a field of wild high ticklish grass
blowing in an almost hysterical wind
and we just start jumping and jumping
crazy jumping
I can't believe how high we are jumping
The earth is a trampoline and I am not afraid
to go higher and higher

When I wake up I think
Oh, this is it. This is justice.

V-DAY

SAY IT, STAGE IT:
V-DAY AT TWENTY

Susan Celia Swan, V-Day Executive Director
Purva Panday Cullman, V-Day Senior Programs Director

Twenty years ago, Eve Ensler's play *The Vagina Monologues* gave birth to V-Day, a global activist movement to end violence against all women and girls. The play and the playwright exploded onto the scene, garnering headlines and rave reviews, filling the theater night after night, breaking taboos, opening spaces for dialogue where they hadn't existed before, and shattering the silence around women's experiences with sexuality and violence. It was pathbreaking. In 2006, *The New York Times* called *The Vagina Monologues* "probably the most important piece of political theater of the last decade," and since that time, it and Eve have received numerous accolades, from an Obie Award to a Tony Award.

The play's boldness—rooted in the experiences of more than two hundred women Eve interviewed—broke through the repression, denial, secrets, shame, and self-hatred that sexual and gender violence have wrought. With humor and empathy, it woke people up. The energy surrounding the play led to the creation of V-Day, in which, every year, people across the planet stage benefit productions of *The Vagina Monologues*—and other artistic works and campaigns—to raise funds and awareness for women and activist groups working to end violence against all women and girls—cisgender, transgender, and gender-nonconforming.

V-Day quickly grew into a mass movement active on every continent. It has become a crucial catalyst in the global fight to stop gender-based violence, attacking the silence—public and private—that allows violence against women to continue and bringing attention to issues of harassment, rape, battery, incest, female genital mutilation, and sex slavery.

V-Day activists have worked tirelessly at a grassroots level to combat rape culture—often in the face of brutal misogynist resistance. V-Day has raised well over $100 million to build safe houses, save lives, change laws, and fund rape crisis centers, domestic violence shelters, and activist groups doing the essential work of ending violence while serving survivors and their families. Connected globally by the movement and the play, V-Day activists have harnessed art and activism at a scale never seen before.

The Vagina Monologues reminds us with each performance that the personal is political, that speaking out can be an act of resistance. Although the sources of violence are diverse, women who have survived describe facing similar challenges. Besides the pain and strength apparent in their stories of survival, we have seen the same themes emerge: indifference of the authorities, familial denial and secrecy, lack of public outrage about the violence that more than one billion women and girls experience, blatant disregard for the most marginalized, and the prevalence and normalization of rape culture.

As we write this, a war on women is under way, and *The Vagina Monologues* is as relevant as ever. Recent reports from the World Health Organization, the Centers for Disease Control and Prevention, and the United Nations confirm that one in three women on the planet will experience physical or sexual violence in her lifetime. That is more than *one billion* women.*

*unwomen.org/en/what-we-do/ending-violence-against-women/facts-and-figures

A global gag rule under U.S. president Donald Trump is assaulting women's bodies, and it will, as the International Women's Health Coalition has said, "reverse decades of progress on reproductive, maternal and child health, leading to an increase in unintended pregnancies, unsafe abortions, and maternal and newborn deaths worldwide."* Unintended pregnancies will contribute to child marriage and the rape of minors, compounding the inequity under which so many women and girls already live.

In the sphere of education, girls are also being left behind. Cultural mores and poverty put school out of reach for many girls, while those who have access to education—from nursery school up through university—are faced with harassment and assault. Talk to students today, and they will tell you of ongoing assault in the school setting and of the impunity and inequity within the justice systems available to them.†

Political instability and armed conflict—fueled by religious, ethnic, nationalist, and economic forces—further escalate the risk of such violence, as rape, battery, and sexual slavery are used as weapons of war. At

*iwhc.org/2017/01/global-gag-rule-trumps-week-one-attack-women

†nytimes.com/2017/07/31/world/australia/shocking-levels-of-sexual-violence-found-on-australian-campuses-report-says.html

the same time, immigration status, racial bias, transphobia and homophobia, and economic inequality keep women in unsafe working conditions, where they often have to endure violence as part of the job. The destabilization of the planet's climate creates insecurity that often leaves women vulnerable to rape and violence after storms and increasingly erratic climate catastrophes.* Whether they are facing harassment or assault or unstable conditions, women are often trapped in these situations because they need to survive and ensure that their families do too.

V-Day's work globally had shown us that in the midst of great trauma is great possibility. Despite the instinct of communities and families to deny the existence of violence, women and girls survive the unthinkable and miraculously find ways to cope, often with little to no support. While these are perilous times, V-Day believes a worldwide cultural shift that could help end forms of violence against women and girls—and address the interconnected issues of race, class, and gender—is within our grasp. Essential to this shift is effectively reframing the conversation about gender-based violence. V-Day began with the stories of women: their experiences and their desire to end vio-

*huffingtonpost.com/entry/climate-change-threat-women-health-security_us_573f5850e4b045cc9a70ecf3 lence and live sexually free lives. We believe that if we listen to women, address the impact of rape culture, and employ an intersectional paradigm, a different consciousness can emerge across the globe.

We never could have imagined what has emerged over these twenty V-years. We have seen women transformed into community and global leaders after having produced the monologues or having stood onstage performing them. We have seen the intersections of social, economic, environmental, and political issues and how violence against women and girls is deeply connected to the global challenges facing our planet today. We have seen that by placing art at the center of their activism, V-Day activists have sustained and grown a movement unlike any other on the planet.

V-Day has filled stadiums and taken a subversive piece of theater to equally important stages—from Madison Square Garden to a clandestine performance in Islamabad, from the steps of the Michigan State House to national parliaments. It has raised support for and shined light on the issues and the systemic inequalities that deeply impact women and marginalized populations, who have historically received fewer resources and even less attention. These issues range widely, from rampant violence against Native American and First Nations women in the United States and Canada to brutal sexual violence in the Democratic

Republic of Congo to police violence and abuse against African American women in the United States. The movement has supported and opened safe houses—true places of community and transformation—around the world, from Afghanistan to Kenya, and taken to the streets, demanding an end to all forms of violence, from Juárez to New Orleans to Manila. It has inspired women and men to rise in solidarity from Havana to Zagreb, on college campuses, in houses of worship and government, in the most unlikely of places. It has brought together activists to strategize at critical times, in the wake of disasters and war. And it has gone always back to our roots—to art—using dance, film, photography, music, and of course theater to activate people at their cores.

Eve Ensler wrote the movement into being with *The Vagina Monologues,* and then set the stage for grassroots leaders, who make the play their own, creating local movements tied to a global vision and network. V-Day's grassroots leaders determine how to address violence in their homes, communities, and institutions. They show up, year after year, doing the hard work of ending violence, on their own terms.

Today, V-Day is an example of how lasting social and cultural change is spread by ordinary people doing extraordinary things. Of how local women best know what their communities need. And of how the collective dimension of art has the power to transform thinking and provoke people to act and serve, galvanizing them in surprising and revolutionary ways.

V-Day lives on a cellular level, in people's hearts and minds. It gains momentum on a grassroots level, in people's individual and collective actions. It is an energy unto itself, outside of any one person's grasp—a catalyst, a movement, an ongoing experiment, a beautiful mystery that only art could create.

V-History

The *V* in V-Day stands for "victory," "valentine," and "vagina." V-Day's work is grounded in four core beliefs.

1. Art has the power to transform thinking and inspire people to act.
2. Lasting social and cultural change is spread by ordinary people doing extraordinary things.
3. Local women know what their communities need and can become unstoppable leaders.
4. We must look at the intersection of class, environmental catastrophe, gender, imperialism, militarism, patriarchy, poverty, racism, and war to fully understand violence against women.

V-Day's activities are designed to attack the silence—public and private—that allows violence against women to continue. V-Day provides a path to action through productions of *The Vagina Monologues* and other works written or curated by Eve Ensler and V-Day (including *Any One of Us: Words from Prison; A Memory, Monologue, a Rant, and a Prayer; I Am an Emotional Creature;* and *Swimming Upstream*). Almost every year since 2002, Eve has written a new Spotlight monologue to address current issues affecting women, updating the V-Day script along the way.

With creativity and vision, V-Day activists around the world increase awareness and raise money to stop violence against women and girls in their own communities and globally. V-Day events have taken place in all fifty states and in more than two hundred countries and territories. Since 1998, thousands upon thousands of V-Day benefit performances have been produced by volunteer activists in the United States and around the world.

These performances are just the beginning. V-Day stages large-scale benefits and produces groundbreaking gatherings, films, and campaigns to educate and to help change social attitudes toward violence against women. In twenty years, the V-Day movement, a 501(c)(3) nonprofit, has raised over $100 million dollars, educating millions about the issue of violence against women and the efforts to end it, crafting international media, educational, and PSA campaigns, and funding more than thirteen thousand community-based anti-violence programs and safe houses in Afghanistan, Congo, Iraq, and Kenya. During this period, *The Vagina Monologues* has been translated into more than forty-eight languages and braille, and has been performed by women of all abilities.

And V-Day has given birth to another social movement—One Billion Rising. Every February 14, we invite the one billion women who have experienced violence—and anyone who wants to show solidarity with them—to rise as one, in a movement of dance to reclaim their bodies and political activism to reclaim their societies. We want to show our local communities and the world what one billion looks like and shine a light on the rampant impunity and injustice that survivors most often face. We rise through dance to express joy and community and celebrate the fact that we have not been defeated by this violence. We rise to show we are determined to create a new kind of consciousness—one where violence will be resisted until it is unthinkable. We rise to envision and bring in a new world.

In the Beginning

In 1994, New York–based playwright, performer, and activist Eve Ensler wrote an honest, heartbreaking, and humorous fictional play based on more than two hundred interviews she conducted with a wide variety of women. The play, *The Vagina Monologues*, was first performed in 1996 by Eve herself, and received instant acclaim, playing to sold-out houses. Eve performed the show for six months in New York, then took it on the road.* After every performance, she was met by countless women who shared their own stories of surviving violence at the hands of relatives, lovers, and strangers. Overwhelmed by the number of women and girls who had experienced violence, and compelled to do something about it, she began to envision *The Vagina Monologues* as more than a provocative work of art; it could be a mechanism for moving people to act to end violence.

Eve, together with a group of New York City–based volunteers, founded V-Day on Valentine's Day 1998. The first V-Day was marked by a star-studded, sold-out benefit performance of *The Vagina Monologues* at the Hammerstein Ballroom in New York City. In just one night, $250,000 was raised and the V-Day move-

*After Eve's run, the play continued for four and a half more years off-Broadway, with a cast of three actors performing the show each night. In order for women onstage to represent the diversity of stories being told and the universality of issues women face, Eve made it a stipulation in her contract that the producers cast women from racially diverse backgrounds. Eve and the producers made an arrangement so that five dollars of every ticket sale would be donated to V-Day, providing the critical resources needed to launch the movement.

ment was born. Three years later, on February 10, 2001, a benefit performance of *The Vagina Monologues* sold out eighteen thousand seats at Madison Square Garden, raising one million dollars. The world was taking notice.

A Campus Movement

Interest ignited on U.S. college campuses, and in 1999 V-Day launched its College Campaign, which invited groups of students to produce and stage benefit performances of *The Vagina Monologues*. Inspired by the play and the mission, thousands of activists quickly emerged: young women and men who were thrust into the roles of gathering people to a cause, addressing groups and media about their events, and leading a team in a public-awareness and fundraising campaign. In that first year, there were sixty-five V-Day campus productions. As with the original off-Broadway production, V-Day encouraged these productions to be diverse in terms of casting and the production team, and, in the spirit of inclusion, asked that no volunteers be turned away. The campaign grew tremendously over the next five years, and by 2007 more than seven hundred colleges registered to participate.

Over the years, the College Campaign has played a significant role in building anti-violence communities on campuses by bringing together engaged, aware, and empowered women and men who are willing to stand up against violence. These activists have introduced lasting programs and activities to their campuses, such as annual weeklong festivals, violence-free zones, and twenty-four-hour speak-outs to stop rape. Students at Arizona State University raised fifteen thousand dollars to open Home Safe, an on-campus sexual violence prevention and education program, and SAFER (Students Active for Ending Rape)—created through V-Day activities on the campus of Columbia University—helped students change campus policies regarding rape prevention and reporting nationwide.

V-Day's dedication to ending sexual violence on college campuses led to the 2008 creation of the Campus Accountability Project (in partnership with SAFER), which was an early contributor to U.S. senators Kirsten Gillibrand and Claire McCaskill's introduction of the Campus Accountability and Safety Act in July 2014. In many ways, the College Campaign has brought a generation of young women and men to envision a new paradigm for social action. It is not uncommon to see V-Day proudly listed in Facebook and LinkedIn profiles and on résumés of recent college graduates. Being part of the V-Day movement signifies a lifelong commitment to justice for women and girls everywhere.

Going Global

As the College Campaign gained momentum, word spread to community activists and local theater and anti-violence groups. As a result, in 2001 the Worldwide Campaign* began to take shape. Just as college students organize benefit performances of *The Vagina Monologues,* so too do communities around the world. Growing from forty-one events in 2001 to hundreds annually today, the campaign comes alive each year through the unrivaled commitment and ingenuity of grassroots activists.

Funds raised by V-Day Community Campaign organizers have stopped the closure of rape crisis centers and many other organizations that work to end violence against women, helped them expand their services, and impacted the judicial process for women. Here are a handful of examples:

- In 2003, the proceeds from a local performance of *The Vagina Monologues* in Nairobi, Kenya, helped reopen a women's shelter that had closed its doors due to lack of funding.
- In rural Borneo, V-Day activism helped ensure that rape cases are now heard in the civil

*The Worldwide Campaign is now known as the Community Campaign.

courts rather than the "native court," so that the rights of survivors are better represented.

- In 2003 in Manila, V-Day events produced by the New Voice Company and Philippine female legislators and congressional representatives for the Philippine Senate and House of Representatives led to the passing of key legislation to combat domestic violence and sex trafficking.
- In 2007, the United States House of Representatives approved a long-awaited measure calling for an apology from Japan to "comfort women," a term that refers to the estimated fifty thousand to two hundred thousand girls and young women from China, Taiwan, Korea, the Philippines, Indonesia, Malaysia, the Netherlands, and East Timor who were abducted and forced into sexual slavery to service the Japanese military in "comfort stations" from 1932 to 1945.
- In 2016, two young founders of a group called Mightee Shero Productions developed and produced a tour of performances of *The Vagina Monologues* in correctional facilities throughout New York City. A cast of former inmates, prison administrators, actors, and activists traveled to five facilities, raising awareness and

support for inmates, culminating in a one-night fundraiser with proceeds supporting the Women's Prison Organization.

- In the same year, activists in Kampala succeeded in presenting the first-ever successful production of *The Vagina Monologues* in Uganda, after attempts had been continually shut down since 2005. Proceeds supported Mifumi, a campaigning group that works to end the practice of bride prices and domestic violence in countryside communities.

Shining a Spotlight

In 2001, working with and at the behest of activists on the ground in Afghanistan, V-Day launched a campaign called Afghanistan Is Everywhere. This initiative provided organizers across the world with news and updates about the experience of women in Afghanistan under the Taliban, which they shared at their events to educate and engage a vast network of communities and audiences. Ten percent of the proceeds from each event, totaling more than $250,000, went to Afghan women's groups, assisting them in opening schools and orphanages and providing education and healthcare.

The success of that campaign evolved into the

annual V-Day Spotlight Campaign. Since Afghanistan Is Everywhere, V-Day Spotlight Campaigns have included Native American and First Nations Women, the Missing and Murdered Women in Juárez, Mexico, the Women of Iraq, the Campaign for Justice to Comfort Women, Women in Conflict Zones (including the women of the eastern Congo), the Women of New Orleans and the Gulf South, Women and Girls in Haiti, Women and Girls in Congo, One Billion Rising, and Violence Against Women in the Workplace; the campaigns have raised hundreds of thousands of dollars for women in these areas and brought the issues they face into the public eye.

Vagina Warriors

V-Day campaigns support the empowerment and leadership of women who are negotiating change within a wide variety of local, social, political, and religious contexts. V-Day's core philosophy recognizes that local activists must take the lead in planning activities for the communities in which they live. It is through the work of these activists that V-Day comes alive across the globe.

V-Day's work to end female genital mutilation (FGM) in the Maasai community in Narok, Kenya, was made possible because one Maasai activist's story connected deeply with—and became an expression of—V-Day's philosophy. Agnes Pareyio started educating young women and girls on the dangers of FGM over nineteen years ago. A deep friendship between Agnes and V-Day turned into a partnership that, in 2002, gave birth to the first V-Day safe house, led by Agnes and her team at the Tasaru Ntomonok Initiative. A place where girls in Narok can go to be educated and live without fear of being cut, the V-Day Safe House for Girls is a monumental success, inspiring women's leaders from across Africa to end FGM on the continent.

In Kabul, V-Day partnered with longtime V-Day activists to support the Promoting Women's Capabilities by Education Center, which provides classes in computer skills, science, English, and literacy to economically disadvantaged local women, many of whom have experienced violence, forced marriage, and depression. Seeking to combat the decades of fundamentalism that has torn down women's autonomy in Afghanistan, the center, which was founded by and is run by Afghan women, provides critical support and information around issues like domestic violence, legal rights, rape within marriage, birth control, and pregnancy.

The Democratic Republic of Congo has, since 1996, endured the deadliest war since World War II. The conflict—a proxy war for Congo's vast natural resources—has directed rampant violence toward raping, mutilating, and murdering women. Advocates on the ground estimate that more than half a million women and girls have been raped since the conflict began.* In addition to the severe psychological impact, sexual and gender violence leaves many survivors with genital lesions, traumatic fistulas, severed and broken limbs, unwanted pregnancies, and sexually transmitted diseases, including HIV. Survivors are regularly ostracized and abandoned by their families and communities. An added challenge is widespread gender inequity.

In 2007, Eve was invited to visit Bukavu, in the eastern Congo, by Dr. Denis Mukwege of Panzi Hospital to witness firsthand the atrocities that women were experiencing in Congo. He had established a hospital to provide emergency medical care during the war, including treatment and surgery for survivors of sexual violence. It was on this trip that Eve met Christine Schuler Deschryver, a tireless activist for the rights of Congolese women. Together they met with dozens of women survivors. It was these women who came up with the idea for a place called the City of Joy, where they could live in community in order to heal—and to *turn their pain into power*. And so, with support from V-Day activists across the world and a group of gener-

*abcnews.go.com/Politics/International/story?id=8305857

ous donors, this dream was made real. Under the leadership of Christine and in partnership with women survivors, construction on the City of Joy began in August 2009, down the road from Panzi Hospital. V-Day opened the City of Joy in February 2011, and the first class of women began in June 2011. Since that time, classes of ninety women, ages eighteen to thirty, have lived at the City of Joy for six-month periods. By the end of 2017, one thousand women had gone through the program and returned to their communities as leaders.

Conceived, owned, and run by Congolese women and men, the center has flourished since it opened its doors. The City of Joy is different from many other traditional NGO direct-service programs. It does not use a sponsorship model, and it does not view the women it serves as individuals who need to be saved; rather, the City of Joy aims to provide women with the opportunity to heal and redirect in a community, on their own terms. Its philosophy is grounded in the following beliefs, which are central to V-Day's work:

- Each woman is unique and valuable to her society, and has a right to be treated with dignity, respect, love, and compassion.
- Women are not broken "victims"; rather they are survivors who have been through unjust gender traumas.

- Each woman is capable of activating her own ability to recover, heal, and be an empowered and transformational leader.
- Rebirth is possible.

The City of Joy's revolutionary Vagina Warrior Program aims to provide a safe and empowering community for survivors of gender violence who have demonstrated leadership qualities. The focus is on healing trauma, building self-esteem and skills, and training women leaders. Women experience a vast range of activities over the course of their stay. From leadership training on rights awareness, the judiciary, community activism, media, and communications to specialized psychosocial care, massage, self-defense, and comprehensive sexuality education, the center prepares women not only to integrate back into their communities with confidence but also to lead. Women graduate having conquered literacy and English, and are exposed to everything from physical education, culinary arts, theater, and dance to craft-making, onsite farming, and agro-pastoral training at V-World Farm, the center's sister program. At the tech center, women learn computer literacy, helping to better prepare them for the current global workplace.

Women leaving the City of Joy have had the opportunity to heal from their emotional wounds, live in a community, recognize their leadership potential, and gain valuable skills they can apply to their lives, future ventures, and engagement in civic life. The transformation is awe-inspiring. In a society that has for the most part rejected women survivors of violence, it is extraordinary to see a group of women so empowered and determined.

Graduates have integrated back into their communities as true leaders, sharing the skills and information they learned at the City of Joy with their peers and families, starting nonprofits including orphanages and homes for the elderly, launching small businesses, leading at the community level, working as journalists and farmers, and returning to school to further their education.

In a *Time* magazine article on rape entitled "The Secret War Crime," survivor, City of Joy graduate and now staff member Jane Mukunilwa was interviewed about the program:

> The therapy, says Mukunilwa, lets women understand that the rape was not their fault. The life skills and leadership training gain them confidence, and the nurturing atmosphere enables them to build support networks that last long after the program finishes. Graduates are expected to establish women's support groups when they go

> home and become leaders in their community. "People think that, after being raped, you are just a victim," says Mukunilwa. "What City of Joy taught me is that life goes on after rape. Rape is not the end. It is not a fixed identity."*

Perhaps more than any other program or campaign, the City of Joy exemplifies what V-Day is all about—community, transformation, and love. It is at once a physical place and a metaphor.

The V-Day Model Expands

As the V-Day movement grew, interest within communities hinted at the success a coordinated V-Day effort in one geographic location could yield, and several groups began to register to hold multiple V-Day events in the same cities. For an inaugural run in V-Day's hometown of New York, Eve and the V-Day team planned a two-week festival of spoken-word, performance, and community events in June 2006 called Until the Violence Stops: NYC. More than one hundred writers and fifty actors donated their talents to create four marquee celebrity events. Seventy local

*time.com/war-and-rape

community events also took place, involving thousands of grassroots activists throughout the city's five boroughs.

One event, an evening entitled *A Memory, a Monologue, a Rant, and a Prayer,* featured original writings by world-renowned authors and playwrights. It was released as a book in May 2007.

The festival also featured a new theatrical piece entitled *Any One of Us: Words from Prison,* a compilation of the writings of incarcerated women, highlighting the connection between women in prison and their past personal experiences with sexual violence. The piece, curated by Eve and Kimberlé Crenshaw, a leading scholar in critical race theory, was an extension of Eve and V-Day's work with incarcerated women over the years. In 2003, the PBS film *What I Want My Words to Do to You* documented writing workshops that Eve conducted with women in Bedford Hills Correctional Facility. The film won the Grand Jury Prize at the 2003 Sundance Film Festival and has been consistently shown at prisons across the country for staff and inmates, as well as wider audiences, since then.

Since the debut of Until the Violence Stops, in New York City, the event model has been replicated in Ohio, Kentucky, Rhode Island, Paris, Los Angeles, and Lima, and the two new artistic pieces have been performed in hundreds of communities around the globe.

V-Day activists worldwide have also screened the documentary, raising funds for prisoners' rights groups.

In 2013, V-Day launched the One Billion Rising for Justice U.S. Prisons Project in conjunction with incarcerated women around the country. The project embraced a restorative rather than punitive justice model and sought to bring higher ethical standards of treatment to the incarcerated population. It also brought attention to issues including racism, poverty, and violence that have led to the incarceration of many women—women of color in particular.

Over the years, many V-Day and One Billion Rising activists created events and actions to support women in prison as part of their local efforts. In 2015, *The New York Times* reported on a performance at the Taconic Correctional Facility in New York State, in which the producer, Elyse Sholk, wrote that the show "affirmed a core belief that drove us to assemble our powerhouse cast in the first place: formerly incarcerated women, professional actresses, and activists are well-positioned to leverage their art and activism to affirm and remind us all that women in prison matter."*

As V-Day's work expanded, Eve created addi-

*nytlive.nytimes.com/womenintheworld/2015/05/25/happy-birthday-eve-ensler tional vehicles through which individuals and communities could address issues surrounding gender and violence. In 2004, the first all-trans-women performance of *The Vagina Monologues* took place in Los Angeles. At the invitation of the cast, Eve wrote a new monologue, "They Beat the Girl Out of My Boy . . . or So They Tried." The piece is now in the official script for V-Day performances and has brought many transgender participants into productions, inspiring participation in other monologues and in various parts of the production process. Proceeds from productions have gone to crucial organizations including the Intersex Society of North America; ASTTeQ (Action Santé Travestis et Transexuels du Québec); Austin Latina/Latino Lesbian, Gay, Bisexual, and Transgender Organization; Indiana Transgender Rights Advocacy Alliance; Louisiana Trans Advocates; Metro Trans Umbrella Group; SUNY Potsdam Lesbian, Gay, Bisexual and Transgender Association; and hundreds of others.

In 2011, V-Girls, a global network of girl activists and advocates, grew out of Eve's play and bestselling book *I Am an Emotional Creature: The Secret Life of Girls*. Rooted in youth-driven activism and led by the vision and strategy of the V-Girls Action Team, groups of girls around the world staged performances of *Emotional Creature* and engaged with an academic curriculum covering girl-related issues ranging from body image to sexual orientation. V-Girls gatherings and productions in cities like Paris, Johannesburg, and New York inspired girls to create art and become active in their communities.

Men have been part of V-Day since its inception. From producing, directing, fundraising, publicity, and website development and design to ushering and supporting the cast, men have been actively involved. After eleven years of projecting women's stories via *The Vagina Monologues,* creating safe spaces for women to acknowledge and often share their own stories, and then witnessing the unstoppable spirit of these sexual violence survivors once they had spoken out, V-Day recognized something crucial. A key part of their work had to be to create similar spaces for men to be open, to share, and to unpack feelings about being victims and/or perpetrators. V-Day created a blog series—launched and curated by author/activist Mark Matousek—and supported V-Men Workshops, led by A Call to Men—an anti-violence organization focused on exploring issues around masculinity—to provide men across the movement with the opportunity to examine the Man Box* in which they are so often trapped and to gather emo-

*ted.com/talks/tony_porter_a_call_to_men

tional strength from one another to begin to lead in ending violence against women. Men have produced and appeared onstage in V-productions of *A Memory, a Monologue, a Rant, and a Prayer* and led Men Rising events, under the One Billion Rising umbrella. Men organized, gathered, and mobilized other men to join the struggle to end violence against women and girls. Using tools like "The Man Prayer"—Eve's new piece written for men to perform—One Billion Rising saw groundbreaking, transformative initiatives led and organized by men, serving as an inspiration for other men around the world to be part of the radical shift in consciousness of how women and girls are treated and seen on the community and global level. Across the years, V-Day has also produced a series of panel discussions foregrounding the voices of male leaders in the discussion.

Amplifying New Voices

The V-Day movement is continually expanding, reflecting the local and global contexts and conversations that activists are having in their communities and amplifying those voices. Over the years—often after having staged *The Vagina Monologues*—many new and longtime activists have developed and staged their own artistic works centering new voices in the conversation around ending violence against women. V-Day has encouraged activists to curate these community stories, creating a new pathway for artistic events that invite local writers, activists, and artists to participate.

In 2017, as part of V-Day and One Billion Rising's shared focus on violence against women in the workplace, V-Day invited activists to platform the voices of women who are experiencing or fighting workplace violence. Activists were encouraged to stage *The Vagina Monologues* or *A Memory, a Monologue, a Rant, and a Prayer* at their place of work—a hospital, factory, or office building—bringing the call for justice, safety, and equality to these sites of violence through the plays, and calling out impunity through a radical artistic production featuring women in their field. As part of this effort, activists were encouraged to invite women facing workplace violence to write testimonials, which were featured in community productions.

Creative Resistance

V-Day shatters taboos, lifts the veil of secrecy from the issue of violence against women, and pushes the edge. While the movement has faced opposition over the years, V-Day has always chosen to speak the truth about violence and women's sexuality. When Eve Ensler first performed *The Vagina Monologues,* even saying the word "vagina" out loud was met with controversy and discomfort. Radio stations refused to allow "vagina" to be said on the air. TV stations ran entire segments on the play without mention of the word, and newspapers hid under the safety of abbreviation. Twenty years later *The Vagina Monologues* has become part of popular culture, and the word "vagina" is spoken openly on TV and radio and printed freely in newspapers and magazines all over the world. With the word being uttered and printed in mainstream media, V-Day has been a catalyst that has helped to shift culture and break through taboos so that women who have suffered invisibly in silence are made visible.

The pushback that V-Day has faced over the years has provided campuses and communities unique opportunities to turn critical feedback into constructive dialogue among students, faculty, and community members. Pushback has also created an environment in which fixed ideas are changed, and in many cases groups end up coming together to support one another in the fight to defend *The Vagina Monologues*. Through acts of creative resistance, productions of the play, and other V-Day campaign activities, activists have defended their right to free speech, to a life free from violence, and to express women's agency over their bodies.

In 2005, Notre Dame University officials banned

the on-campus production of *The Vagina Monologues,* sparking wide-ranging debate and resulting in a panel discussion at the university featuring members of the faculty and Eve. The following year, Notre Dame president Rev. John I. Jenkins announced that he would allow the campus production, stating, "The creative contextualization of a play like *The Vagina Monologues* can bring certain perspectives on important issues into a constructive and fruitful dialogue with the Catholic tradition. This is a good model for the future."*

At the same time, the Ugandan government shut down a production of *The Vagina Monologues* in Kampala despite the scrutiny of the international press. Amid the discussion that ensued, activists responding to this controversy were still able to raise eleven thousand dollars for the Lira Women Peace Initiative and Kitgum Women Peace Initiative, two local groups working to keep women safe in northern Uganda.

In 2006, V-Day again found itself the center of controversy when the president of Providence College banned the annual production of *The Vagina Monologues*. Hundreds protested, and V-Day organizers from across Rhode Island (as well as many of the event's beneficiaries) came to the aid of the Providence Col-

*Margaret Fosmoe, "ND Discourse Ends: 'Monologues' Allowed," *South Bend Tribune,* April 5, 2006.

lege organizers, helping to arrange an off-campus production. Following the outpouring of community support, the production has continued to take place at the college ever since.

Now, in the aftermath of the 2016 U.S. presidential campaign and in the midst of the presidency of Donald Trump, *The Vagina Monologues* feels as topical as ever, as the country and the world are alight with conversations about consent, sexual harassment, and assault. Journalist Sarah Rebell, who spoke to V-Day activists in red and swing states in the U.S., wrote, "Many said how empowering it has been to have *The Vagina Monologues* as an outlet, a means of expressing their anger about the current political situation. It's also been a way of connecting with their larger communities, of promoting empathy and inclusiveness in a potentially bleak and divisive time."*

By generating media coverage and starting a worldwide dialogue, V-Day activists have addressed opposition to their work, turning controversy into conversations and ultimately reaching a deeper understanding about the experiences of women with sexuality and violence, creating the very change V-Day seeks. They have learned to fight for what they want most.

*theintervalny.com/features/2017/02/v-day-in-trumpland-exploring-the-relevance-of-the-vagina-monologues

On April 11–12, 2008, V-Day celebrated its tenth anniversary, V to the Tenth, in New Orleans, to shine a light on the issues facing the Gulf South community in the wake of Hurricanes Katrina and Rita, which devastated the region. Over the weekend, V-Day took over the New Orleans Arena and Louisiana Superdome, which served as a makeshift shelter during Hurricane Katrina and came to symbolize the lack of care for the poor and the African American community. More than thirty thousand people attended the events over the two days, and V-Day transformed the Superdome into "SUPERLOVE," with conversations, slam poetry, performances, storytelling, and art that explored the issues of the environment, failing infrastructure, and violence against women with an intersectional lens. Thousands traveled from out of state and overseas for events that featured more than 125 speakers and 40 stars, a choir of 200, and 800-plus volunteers.

V-Day's Coastal Women Coming Home Project brought twelve hundred women displaced by the hurricanes to New Orleans for the weekend and provided access to free massage, support groups, yoga, meditation, and makeovers. As part of SUPERLOVE, V-Day staged the premier reading of *Swimming Upstream,* written by fifteen local New Orleans artists in partnership

V • D A Y

with the Ashé Cultural Arts Center. The play told the raw stories of women who lived through Hurricane Katrina with grace, rage, humor, and great resiliency.

A benefit performance of *The Vagina Monologues* featured Jane Fonda, Rosario Dawson, Kerry Washington, Ali Larter, Calpernia Addams, Lilia Aragón, Stéphanie Bataille, Jennifer Beals, Ilene Chaiken, Didi Conn, Lella Costa, Alexandra Hedison, Shirley Knight, Kristina Krepela, Christine Lahti, Liz Mikel, Doris Roberts, Daniela Sea, Amber Tamblyn, Leslie Townsend, and Monique Wilson, plus musical performances by Faith Hill, Jennifer Hudson, Peter Buffett, Charmaine Neville, and the Voices of New Orleans Gospel Choir.

V-Day donated more than $700,000 to groups in the region working to end violence against women and girls.

The V to the Tenth celebrations were an important marker for the V-Day movement, laying the groundwork for an intensive multiyear focus on women survivors of violence in Congo and for a series of events, conversations, and actions around different forms of violence marginalized communities experience—from economic to environmental to racial. It was out of this work that the One Billion Rising campaign was born, an annual global action demanding an end to all forms of violence against women.

Bodies moving spontaneously, but not randomly, are participating in a global conversation about violence. And in dancing at the sites that the Risers select, the risings tell us something about intersectional politics the world over. People—women—live intersectionally—sites where sexism overlaps with economic marginality, racism, environmental degradation, queerphobia, able-ism, xenophobia, and the like. Risers show us what the face of intersectionality is by what they choose to resist. [There are] thousands of unique actions that make up the global mapping of how violence festers at the intersections of vulnerability. Dancing at these sites calls attention to these vulnerabilities, and transforms them into sites of resistance. It is coalitional politics on a global scale.

—Kimberlé Crenshaw, co-founder of the African American Policy Forum, professor of law at UCLA, faculty director of the Center for Intersectionality and Social Policy Studies at Columbia Law School, and V-Day board member

Launched on Valentine's Day 2012, One Billion Rising began as a call to action based on the staggering statistic that one in three women on the planet will be beaten or raped during her lifetime. With the world population at seven billion, this adds up to more than *one billion* women and girls.

On V-Day's fifteenth anniversary, February 14, 2013, people across the world came together to express their outrage, strike, dance, and rise in defiance of the injustices women suffer, demanding an end at last to sexual and physical violence. As One Billion Rising has grown and the local campaigns have deepened, the scope of issues igniting grassroots activism has expanded. One Billion Rising activists are seeking justice in the face of economic violence; racial violence; gender violence; violence caused by corruption, occupation, and aggression; violence caused by environmental disasters, climate change, and environmental plunder; violence impacting women in the context of state-sponsored wars, militarization, and the worsening internal and international displacement of millions of people; and violence created by capitalist greed.

Through One Billion Rising, activists have mobilized, engaged, and awakened people worldwide, making violence against women a global human issue not restricted to country or tribe or class or religion. They have revealed it as a patriarchal mandate, present in every culture of the world. They have made visible the volatile connections between violence against women and economic, environmental, racial, and gender injustice. They have formed new and lasting coalitions between existing groups and individuals not only within the women's movement but also between people's movements covering diverse sectors. And they have shown that there is nothing more powerful than global solidarity, as it makes all of us safer in our outspokenness, braver in what we feel willing to do.

One Billion Rising has demonstrated the power of art and dance and the astonishing political alchemy that occurs when art and activism happen simultaneously. Dance is one of the most powerful forces on the earth, and we have only just begun to tap into where it can take us. The struggle of humanity is the struggle to return to our bodies. Through trauma, cruelty, shame, oppression, violence, rape, and exclusion, the human species has been wounded, and we have been forced to flee our bodies. This same cruelty, rape, and oppression have been enacted on the earth itself, and the consequences have been dire.

Dancing allows us to come back into our bodies as individuals and groups. It allows us to go further, to include everyone, to tap into a revolutionary and poetic energy that is inviting us to take the lid off the patriarchal container, releasing more of our wisdom, our self-love. Our sexuality, our compassion, and fierceness. Dancing is defiance. It is joyous and raging. It is contagious and free and beyond corporate or state control. We have only begun to dance.

The intentional structure of One Billion Rising—based on the idea of "expanding and not branding"—has allowed for mass engagement across sectors and existing networks that have traditionally worked apart from one another, while also providing a platform to honor and recognize the incredible work already being done on the ground by groups fighting to end gender-based violence. In many ways, One Billion Rising is an energy that moved across the planet, a decision shared by activists and adapted to each culture and place. From unions, migrant workers, and teachers to religious leaders, actors, and youth, the campaign has inspired countless individuals to take to the streets. Activists have brought to the surface the intersection of issues both causing and affecting violence against women.

Rising activists have supported and taken part in Say Her Name actions—which call for an end to the scandalous ignoring of violence against African American women—and called for a gender-inclusive movement to end state violence and uplift the stories of black women. Through the frame of Artistic Uprising, many participants stage artistic and political events—in locations throughout the United States and the world—centering on creative resistance and voice, and the power of art to engage wide support for cultural change.

Groups that have been traditionally marginalized—including indigenous, LGBTQ+, disabled, migrant, and incarcerated women—are at the center of the campaign in many communities. One Billion Rising has created global solidarity and strength, cutting across borders, races, religions, sexual orientations, ages, genders, and abilities. It has also reignited solidarity between women's organizations in various countries and has rekindled the ethos of sisterhood among women on a global scale.

One Billion Rising has affirmed what a global solidarity movement looks like—people coming together for a uniquely local yet shared global vision. One such example is the recent Women Workers Rising effort, a coalition calling for broad-based solidarity among women workers, an end to workplace violence and harassment, pay equity, a fair living wage, paid leave, and labor rights.

As One Billion Rising has been embraced by veteran and new activists alike, V-Day has seen its work go deeper into the fabric of communities, helping to provide a path for groups to come together and catalyzing V-Day into a new place in its evolution as a global grassroots movement.

It all started with a series of stunning monologues, but it has turned into an energetic, determined global uprising, crisscrossing continents, demanding one thing—liberation for all our sisters. As V-Day enters its twentieth year, we continue to seek a world where women and girls will thrive rather than merely survive. We invite you to join us.

V-DAY MISSION STATEMENT

VDAY

V-Day is an organized response against violence toward women.

V-Day is a vision: We see a world where women live safely and freely.

V-Day is a demand: Rape, incest, battery, genital mutilation, and sexual slavery must end now.

V-Day is a spirit: We believe women should spend their lives creating and thriving rather than surviving or recovering from terrible atrocities.

V-Day is a catalyst: By raising money and consciousness, it will unify and strengthen existing anti-violence efforts. Triggering far-reaching awareness, it will lay the groundwork for new educational, protective, and legislative endeavors throughout the world.

V-Day is a process: We will work as long as it takes. We will not stop until the violence stops.

V-Day is a day: We proclaim Valentine's Day as V-Day, to celebrate women and end the violence.

V-Day is a fierce, wild, unstoppable movement and community. Join us!

THE 10 GUIDING PRINCIPLES OF CITY OF JOY

Like all communities, the City of Joy has its own culture, one that is grounded in love and respect for one another and the unique experiences each woman brings to the table.

1. Tell the truth.
2. Stop waiting to be rescued; take initiative.
3. Know your rights.
4. Raise your voice.
5. Share what you've learned.
6. Give what you want the most.

7. Feel and tell the truth about what you've been through.
8. Use it to fuel a revolution.
9. Practice kindness.
10. Treat your sister's life as if it were your own.

For more information, visit:

VDay.org

OneBillionRising.org

CityOfJoyCongo.org

Facebook.com/vday

Twitter: @Vday

Instagram: @vdayorg

AFTERWORD

Monique Wilson, Director, One Billion Rising

On February 14, 2013, I found myself in front of a crowd of thousands in Manila as they danced for One Billion Rising. As I looked out from the stage, I couldn't help but think back to the play and movement that brought me to that moment. Grassroots women leaders and groups, workers, migrant families, teachers, urban poor women, women from marginalized communities, indigenous women, Muslim sisters, members of the LGBTQI community, all were dancing and singing so defiantly and passionately for freedom from violence and poverty. They moved me.

I was also moved because I knew that all over the Philippines—and in more than two hundred other countries—there were equally incredible risings taking place that day. I was moved because it took me back to thirteen years before, when together with other activists I first brought *The Vagina Monologues* and the V-Day movement to the Philippines. The memories, struggles, victories, journeys—both political and personal—came rushing back in that moment. In images like myriad colors of light, I saw every step of our journey in the women's fierceness, courage, generosity, and love for one another and our country, as well as in their joy and their insistence on hope. Every victory, every challenge, every deepening of love and sisterhood—spinning in radiant colors that illumined an astounding journey—had arrived at this moment.

After acting since I was nine years old and creating a feminist political theater company at twenty-four, I produced Eve Ensler's *The Vagina Monologues* in 2000 in the Philippines, Hong Kong, Singapore, and Japan, because I believe theater shouldn't just entertain but should also awaken, incite, inspire, educate, and transform. Even in those early years, I felt that we could not do the play simply as artists, that we had to partner with the women's movement, with our grassroots women's groups, to contextualize the play for us in the Philippines and for our migrant groups everywhere, to give it connection and meaning. I invited GABRIELA—a national alliance of two hundred women's groups and the most political, militant, anti-imperialist grassroots women's movement in the Philippines—to partner with us from the moment we were birthing the play in the Philippines and around Asia. For many years I had struggled to find a way to marry my art and activism, but then *The Vagina Monologues* and V-Day came along and fundamentally changed the course of my life.

When *The Vagina Monologues* opened in the Philippines, a strange phenomenon began to unfold. Filipinos were welcoming and receptive, despite being engulfed in a dominant patriarchal society fraught with religious and cultural barriers. Political and social shifts transpired very quickly.

As we began to perform *The Vagina Monologues*—or *Usaping Puki,* in Filipino—fifteen years ago, in cities and villages across the Philippines and within Filipino migrant communities abroad, the response from the audience was diverse and unexpected. Filipinos of all ages, classes, educational and economic backgrounds, and religions watched the play and discussed it intensely. It didn't matter if the setting was a theater venue, a stadium, a conference room, a classroom, a field, or an open-air park—the reactions were consistent. After all, it was not every day in Philippine culture that the word "vagina" or the issues of women's empowerment and women's rights—or even women's desires—came up. As the play was opening, Filipina women did not even have legal protection from sex trafficking, domestic violence, or marital rape. Currently, because we are one of the largest Catholic countries in the world, reproductive health laws are still being fought for, and divorce does not exist. It was not just the profound humanity of the play, or its humor or poignancy, that seemed to alternately unnerve and entertain Filipina women; what I think disturbed them more were the questions the play raised for them: questions about the worth of women; the double standards in culture, laws, and rights between men and women; and the deeply entrenched silence that surrounded issues of violence, justice, and empowerment—a silence that the play smashed.

At the performances, you could feel a different kind of energy emerging. *The Vagina Monologues* ushered something new into our predominantly conservative country. What the play first gave us was the language of truth—the language of the exposed realities that were reflected in the narratives. Perhaps because centuries of corruption brought on by colonization by the West have permeated the Filipino way of life, the Filipino people had gotten used to masking the truth rather than exposing it.

The play touched, affected, awakened, and disturbed, particularly for an audience whose cultural norm was to not speak openly about sexuality. For many Filipina women, the play became a poetry of consciousness, of desire, truth, and empowerment. The play awakened literal and metaphoric experiences for us. We also saw, as theater practitioners and political activists, that the stories in the monologues—while not specifically about the Philippines—could be universally understood, allowing the play to be received uniquely in every community, regardless of its specific cultural, religious, and political contexts. This began a profound process of personal awakening leading to a societal and national transformation.

For us in the Philippines, the word "vagina" became a source of power because it had never been spoken so openly and so proudly before, especially in the face of church teachings that continue to reinforce patriarchal structures meant to silence women and deny them their sexual power and rights. In the Philippine language there is no biological word for "vagina," only a derogatory term. When you do not have a name for your vagina, how can you speak about being raped, trafficked, incested, or sold into sexual slavery? The continued denial of women's access to their voices and bodies perpetuates the subjugation and oppression of women. Thus the play gave true empowerment to women who had been denied their most basic of rights.

The play broke barriers because the stories celebrated a woman for her desires, her conditions, and her needs, and did not classify her by class, religion, identity, or race. The all-encompassing culture of silence was threatened.

In February 2001, outside the theater where the play was running in Manila, our partner GABRIELA organized national rallies calling for the resignation of President Joseph Estrada; his state of the nation address a few months earlier had not mentioned prevailing women's issues in the Philippines, the most common of which were incest, domestic violence, battery, sex trafficking, and rape. GABRIELA provided information on its advocacy work in the promotions for the play, and help desks were set up in the theater lobby, where women experiencing any kind of abuse could go for advice and information after the show. They also brought us deep into grassroots communities.

Partnering with the grassroots women's movement helped us view their situations through a lens that analyzes violence against women from a sociopolitical perspective. The founding member of GABRIELA and one of the country's leading feminists, Mother Mary John Mananzan, Order of St. Benedict, describes the "woman question" in the Philippines as the "phenomenon of the discrimination, subordination, exploitation, and oppression of women." She describes feminism in the Philippine context as not only "an understanding of the woman question" but also as "working toward a systematic change, a change in perspective, change in structure, and change in values in the most comprehensive and inclusive manner."* So for us in the Philippines, *The Vagina Monologues* lent to not only understanding and awareness of the "woman question" but also to a commitment to vanquish all forms of violence against women in our society.

Hearing the untold stories of abuse and inequality in the play reinforced a need to take responsibility and be accountable for our part in the cycle of violence—as victim/survivor, spectator, or perpetrator. This is where the inclusion of the "woman question" perspective made and continues to make *The Vagina Monologues* very persuasive in the Philippines. With the play, theater became and continues to be an important medium to enhance the vision and work of the women's movement, and has also become an important tool to raise consciousness and funds and put radical and transformative actions into place.

*Sr. Mary John Mananzan, *The Woman Question in the Philippines.* Manila: Institute of Women's Studies, 1997, 33–34.

In producing the play and mounting V-Day events all around the Philippines, Hong Kong, Singapore, and Japan in the succeeding years, we placed our political issues firmly at the forefront of each production: sex trafficking, justice for comfort women (the first sex slaves of World War II), militarization, and migrant issues, among many others. In partnership with GABRIELA, we used the play not only to empower women but also to place the stories of the play in context with our own issues as Southeast Asian women, long subjugated and exploited by both Western states and our own governments. The play became an important advocacy tool to raise awareness of violence against women and the national and international policies that were keeping that violence in place.

Our journey was not without challenges. In the beginning, the media would not print the word "vagina," and TV and radio shows would not allow us to say the word to promote the show—a definite problem considering the play's title. No sponsors would touch us. The Catholic Church raised much opposition to our productions, and in a country where militant political leaders get arbitrarily arrested, detained, and tortured by our police and military, there were always huge risks. But the power of the play brought the audiences in, and our belief in the merging of the play with our own women's movement gave another platform for our grassroots women to raise their voices.

My own political and social education also deepened in this V-Day journey with GABRIELA. It exposed me to all the forms of violence we women face culturally, physically, politically, and economically. It brought me to the poorest and most marginalized communities in the Philippines to perform the play, which consistently heightened my political consciousness.

There are so many moments that stand out in my memory over the seventeen years of doing the play. In 2000, I was invited to the Women's International War Crimes Tribunal on Japan's Military Sexual Slavery to perform "My Vagina Was My Village." Doing the piece in front of 250 former comfort women from all over Asia was the deepest honor, but it also terrified me. How would I perform a monologue on the very form of rape that the women sitting in front of me had experienced daily for years during World War II—and for which they never received justice? How would I honor the stories of the comfort women who were connected to this piece? For me it was a defining moment—a realization that this was not just a monologue, not just a play, but also a huge and powerful catalyst for awareness and justice.

Another memory is of performing the same piece in 2001 at the first convention of the International League of Peoples' Struggle (ILPS) in Utrecht, in the

Netherlands, where radical militant, anti-imperialist people's groups from around the world gathered to create and envision the charter of ILPS. Workers, migrants, and some of the most marginalized communities present asked me to perform because they said they felt the piece united us as people of the world, connecting our stories and our struggles and highlighting how imperialism creates and escalates violence toward women.

In 2002, after Eve Ensler had graced our V-Day event in Manila in front of six thousand people, women legislators—led by former GABRIELA secretary general Liza Maza—invited us to perform the play in the Philippine congress and senate. The purpose was to enlighten the male legislators about domestic violence and sex trafficking bills that had been lying dormant for close to ten years. Shortly after, the bills were passed. For the legislators, hearing the real experiences of women being violated was a different experience from reading statistical data on violence against women. The play made the experiences more real, more tangible, forcing them to act urgently on what they heard.

In 2003, we performed at the Armed Forces of the Philippines military camp—in the belly of the beast—to highlight the issues of militarism and state-instigated violence. And we asked all the soldiers, the generals, and their wives to watch. I will never forget Lola Narcisa—one of our former comfort women—giving them a fiery, emotional speech on the continued abuse women suffered at the hands of men in power and in uniform, as a hundred Filipina artists and activists sat around her. The army sat in the audience, stunned—perhaps hearing for the first time what violence does to a woman. Just as important was seeing a community of women up there on the stage in solidarity with Lola Narcisa.

In Hong Kong, Singapore, Japan, and London, where we performed the play for migrant women, you could hear audible crying from the audience, and the women, mostly domestic workers, would share their stories after the play, sensing an opening to speak up about their experiences of abuse. Now it is no longer artists performing the play in these communities but domestic workers themselves, using their performances to highlight the issues of forced labor, labor exploitation and abuse, and modern-day slavery.

In 2006, at the trial for the rape of "Nicole," a Filipina woman, by Daniel Smith, a U.S. serviceman, as the guilty verdict was read the court clerk repeatedly mentioned the word "vagina" as the desecrated source of humanity and dignity. A Philippine senator who had once questioned me for doing a play that she thought was "vulgar" sat beside me in the courtroom and thanked me for bringing the play to the Philippines. She said she had never thought the moment would come in the history of our predominantly Catholic country when vaginas, and the violence being done to them, would be spoken about so openly in court; it helped give weight and severity to the case to hear how mutilated and lacerated the girl's vagina was from the rape. She said it was the first time in any court case where the word had been mentioned, and that the play had helped shape national consciousness about removing the shame and stigma associated with saying it.

Currently the play is being performed by youth survivors of Typhoon Haiyan in Tacloban City, and productions are being planned by indigenous women, urban poor women, women farmers, sex workers, and trafficked teachers, all to highlight the various forms of economic, physical, and sexual abuse they suffer.

These are only a few snapshots of an incredible seventeen-year journey with the play, which naturally led to the next level of our advocacy—One Billion Rising, a movement that escalates our demand to end violence toward women and girls. One Billion Rising is the radical child of *The Vagina Monologues* and V-Day. It uses art and activism not only to awaken, educate, and inspire but also to incite, resist, and disrupt. It brings together the deeper interconnected issues of race, economics, class, environment, and war under the lens of "solidarity" and "exploitation," and through the frame of revolutionary change.

Today, *The Vagina Monologues* not only continues to be performed everywhere from major cities and colleges in the Philippines to Filipino migrant and domestic worker communities around the world; it is also completely integrated into our risings. The vagina as both metaphor and theme, the exploration of the "woman question," and the need to use specific, imperative lenses to create change are what connect the play and V-Day to One Billion Rising, continuing its relationship to our women's movement.

For Filipinos, *The Vagina Monologues* has challenged and changed the deeply patriarchal symbolic orders of our society. For us in the Philippines, and in our work within the women's movement, there is no doubt that the play challenges every political and social framework that denies a woman access to her desires, whether they be sexual, emotional, mental, physical, economic, religious, or cultural. The play and its daughter movements have challenged centuries of oppression, allowing us to question and defy deeply entrenched social and political ideologies.

In the Philippines, the play has become the language of defiance, liberation, and expression—and through it, we are able to connect the differences and similarities of our shared experiences, and to articulate them in the contexts of our cultures, histories, and traditions. After centuries of entrenched colonization from the West, the play has given us the power to never again deny ourselves the language of desire, aspirations, dreams, rage, anger, lust, love, joy, and sexuality. We will never again allow the suppression of the subversive revolutionary language of our bodies. We have used and continue to use the play for social transformation and liberation, an important tool for the work of our people's movements. The play's deep-rooted relationship to grassroots movements enhances, ignites, and fuels the difficult, everyday work of eliminating violence.

Growing up artistically and politically because of *The Vagina Monologues* and V-Day was like rising into a glittering consciousness of awakening and empowerment, ascending into the transformative realms of hope and possibility. The experience of being shaken from the deepest slumber because of the play—and then fired into such a profound belief in the power of women, in people, and in the world because of the movements it birthed—reared me from artist to political activist. It is only the highest form of art that insists we not only discover our own realities but also transform them beyond what we are expected and conditioned to accept.

For me, for the people of the Philippines, *The Vagina Monologues* was the catalyst, the root—and the elixir—for the political revolutionary language of the body. From the stage, it continues to bring us into searing truths that penetrate and crystallize inside every pore of our beings, calling us to live to our own deserving and to step into the truth of our value as women. It did this for me, and I have seen how it has done the same for my sisters, not only here but around the world. It reminds us to put our own dignity and worth in the foreground and leads us to trust the depth of who we are and who we deserve to be—not just personally but as a community. One Billion Rising is the play's next powerful portal of transformation, pushing us to go further, be braver, stronger, and louder together than ever before. This alchemy of art, body, and revolution is pushing us into the deepest embodiment and celebration of the most revolutionary act of all: to honor and live fully in our bodies. And through our bodies, to be surrendered alive and awake into creative rebellion, resistance, and disruption so that we can RISE, and keep RISING, into the radical acts of service and love.

ACKNOWLEDGMENTS FOR THE 20TH ANNIVERSARY EDITION

Charlotte Sheedy for the depth of her wisdom, kindness, and care and for being with me on this journey for over forty years.

Jacqueline Woodson for a truly beautiful, generous foreword.

Monique Wilson for the depth of her commitment to this play and this movement, for her beloved friendship and huge heart, and for a soaring afterword.

Susan Celia Swan for twenty years of her devotion, brilliance, and commitment, and for writing such a powerful story of V-Day for this volume.

Purva Panday Cullman for her singular devotion to this play and this movement and for her wonderful words and insights here.

Kimberlé Crenshaw and Johann Hari for their brilliant minds.

Colleen Carroll and Anju Kasturiraj for great work on this edition.

Tony Montenieri for simply making everything possible with his angel heart and enormous talent.

Emily Hartley for making this edition happen with ease, insight, and enthusiasm.

ABOUT THE AUTHOR

PHOTO: © BRIGITTE LACOMBE

EVE ENSLER is an internationally bestselling author and Tony Award–winning playwright whose theatrical works include the Obie Award–winning *The Vagina Monologues,* as well as *Necessary Targets, The Good Body,* and *Emotional Creature*. She is the author of the political memoir *Insecure at Last,* the *New York Times* bestseller *I Am an Emotional Creature,* and a critically acclaimed memoir, *In the Body of the World,* which she has adapted for the stage and will premiere at Manhattan Theatre Club in 2018. Ensler is the founder of V-Day, the global movement to end violence against women and girls that has raised more than $100 million for local groups and activists. She is also the founder of One Billion Rising, the biggest global mass action campaign to end violence against women in human history, which is active in more than two hundred countries, and the co-founder of the City of Joy, the revolutionary leadership center for survivors of gender violence in the Democratic Republic of Congo.

eveensler.org

ABOUT THE TYPE

This book was set in Arrus, a typeface designed by Richard Lipton and first released in 1991. Arrus is based on Lipton's own hand-lettered calligraphic alphabets, which draw their influence from classic inscriptional forms.